Mindful Practice for Social Justice

This book is designed to help you bring mindfulness and social justice to the forefront of your education practice, so you can work toward self-actualization and social transformation. Author Raquel Ríos offers instructional practices, coaching strategies and implementation tools to help you activate mind, body and spirit on your journey to making real changes toward equity in your school or classroom.

What's inside:

♦ Chapter 1 explains the importance of realizing one's powers and how power increases when we discover its purpose and utility in society.

♦ Chapter 2 introduces you to the three domains of Peak Learning Experience (Personal, Social and Transpersonal) that lead to the targeted practices of Authentic Presence, Freedom and Emergence and discusses how bias can limit our ability to see the truth in people and situations.

♦ Chapters 3–5 delve into each domain, offering strategies, activities, reflection questions and application to practice tools.

♦ Chapter 6 discusses the importance of building the right team and the need to change how we recruit talent if we want to innovate our profession.

With the powerful reflection tools and activities in this book, you and your teams will feel more equipped and supported on your path toward mindfulness, social justice and change in education.

Raquel Ríos, PhD, is an educator, learning designer and consultant. She is the author of the book *Teacher Agency for Equity: A Framework for Conscientious Engagement* (Routledge, 2017).

D1559065

Also Available from Routledge
Eye On Education
(www.routledge.com/k-12)

Teacher Agency for Equity:
A Framework for Conscientious Engagement
Raquel Ríos

Confronting White Privilege Within and
Beyond the Classroom:
Tools for Inspiration and Action
Jamila Lyiscott

Let's Get Real:
Exploring Race, Class, and Gender Identities
in the Classroom
Martha Caldwell and Oman Frame

Culturally Relevant Teaching in the English
Language Arts Classroom:
A Guide for Teachers
Sean Ruday

Determining Difference from Disability:
What Culturally Responsive Teachers Should Know
Gerald McCain and Megan Farnsworth

Implicit Bias in Schools:
A Practitioner's Guide
Gina Laura Gullo, Kelly Capatosto, and Cheryl Staats

Anti-Bias Education in the Early Childhood Classroom:
Hand in Hand, Step by Step
Katie Kissinger

Mindful Practice for Social Justice

A Guide for Educators
and Professional Learning
Communities

Raquel Ríos

Routledge
Taylor & Francis Group

NEW YORK AND LONDON

First published 2019
by Routledge
52 Vanderbilt Avenue, New York, NY 10017

and by Routledge
2 Park Square, Milton Park, Abingdon, Oxon, OX14 4RN

*Routledge is an imprint of the Taylor & Francis Group, an
informa business*

Library of Congress Cataloging-in-Publication Data
Names: Ríos, Raquel, author.
Title: Mindfulness and social justice in practice: a guide for
educators and professional learning communities / Raquel Rios.
Description: New York: Routledge, 2019. | Includes
bibliographical references.
Identifiers: LCCN 2018054960 (print) | LCCN 2019003621 (ebook) |
ISBN 9780429199240 (ebook) | ISBN 9780367189242 (hbk) |
ISBN 9780367189259 (pbk) | ISBN 9780429199240 (ebk)
Subjects: LCSH: Affective education. | Mindfulness (Psychology) |
Social justice. | Professional learning communities.
Classification: LCC LB1072 (ebook) | LCC LB1072 .R56
2019 (print) | DDC 370.15/34—dc23
LC record available at https://lccn.loc.gov/2018054960

ISBN: 978-0-367-18924-2 (hbk)
ISBN: 978-0-367-18925-9 (pbk)
ISBN: 978-0-429-19924-0 (ebk)

Typeset in Palatino
by codeMantra

For Marco and Natalia

For Pedro Albizu Campos

Contents

Meet the Author. ix
Acknowledgments x

Introduction. 1

1 You are Either Magical, Or You Are Not. 9
What is Your Power?. 10
Barriers and Limitations to Power 14
Getting Started: Initial Self-Assessment. 15

2 Three Domains for Peak Learning Experience. 21
Overview of Authentic Presence 24
Overview of Freedom. 25
Overview of Emergence. 27
Becoming Aware of Human Experience 28
Implicit Bias Revisited 32

**3 Authentic Presence: Personal Awareness and
    Self-Mastery**. 35
Strategy 1. Contemplation and Meditation 36
Strategy 2. Movement and Yoga 46
Strategy 3. Identity and Culture Study 53
Strategy 4. Acting and Performance. 58
Assessing for Barriers 63
Application to Practice: Planning Tool. 65

4 Freedom: Social Awareness and Adaptability. 69
Strategy 1. Intergroup Dialogue 70
Strategy 2. Rituals and Ceremony. 76
Strategy 3. Balanced Technology. .83
Strategy 4. Bearing Witness 90
Assessing for Barriers 95
Application to Practice: Observation Tool. 97

5   Emergence: Transpersonal Awareness and Agency. . 103
Strategy 1. Envisioning and Imagination. 104
Strategy 2. Wisdom Traditions and Philosophy 110
Strategy 3. Shared Mindful Inquiry 118
Shared Mindful Inquiry Instructions 122
Strategy 4. Channeling Energy 124
Assessing for Barriers 132
Application to Practice: Performance Assessment
    and Coaching Tool 134

6   The Unicorn Point 137
Building a Team. 139

Afterword 141

Meet the Author

Raquel Ríos, PhD is an educator, learning designer, consultant and author of the book, Teacher Agency for Equity: A Framework for Conscientious Engagement (Routledge, 2017). She started her career as a Spanish teacher and has worked nationally in the US and internationally in Spain, the United Arab Emirates and Puerto Rico. She has a PhD in Educational Leadership-K-12, an MS in Elementary Education and a BS in Secondary Foreign Language Education. Her scholarship focuses on teacher education, language and literacy, social justice pedagogy, instructional leadership and mindfulness. Most recently, Dr. Ríos worked at New Teacher Center, a national resource on mentoring and coaching for teacher effectiveness located in Santa Cruz, California. There, she was a key contributor to the redesign of their curriculum and products infusing equity, social-emotional learning and ELA standards aligned instruction. Dr. Ríos writes and consults on topics related to education and her philosophy of conscientious engagement. She lives in New York with her husband, two children and their fish, Mr. Anderson.

Acknowledgments

I wish to thank Lauren Davis for her foresight and the Taylor & Francis editorial team for bringing this work to the public. Thanks to Jeanine Furino for her professionalism and attention to this project. Special thanks to my father for his financial support during the writing of this manuscript, to my husband for his unwavering belief in my life's work and to all the creative and spiritual guides in my family. Lastly, I'd like to express gratitude to all those who closed a door leading me here, to this wide open window.

Introduction

There is an old Cherokee legend in which a grandfather is teaching his grandson about life. It goes like this:

"A fight is going on inside me," he said to the boy. "It is a terrible fight and it is between two wolves. One is evil – he is anger, envy, sorrow, regret, greed, arrogance, self-pity, guilt, resentment, inferiority, lies, false pride, superiority, and ego." He continued, "The other is good – he is joy, peace, love, hope, serenity, humility, kindness, benevolence, empathy, generosity, truth, compassion, and faith. The same fight is going on inside you – and inside every other person, too." The grandson thought about it for a minute and then asked his grandfather, "Which wolf will win?" The old Cherokee simply replied, "The one you feed."[1]

According to Native American medicine, teachers are members of the wolf clan. Wolves are tremendously loyal animals who know how to mark their territory. Recognized as forerunners with keen instincts, they are independent and free but also care for their offspring. When we think about a wolf, we see it howling at the moon. Some say wolves are tapping into the moon's psychic energy.[2] If teaching and guiding others is central to your life's purpose, whether through the practice of education or another serving profession, then you are committed to a life of search and surrender, curiosity and empathy, sensing and leading.

This book is a wolf guide. It is designed to help you bring mindfulness and social justice to the forefront of your practice for self-actualization and social transformation. When a wolf taps into the moon's psychic energy, it is looking to nature for awareness and wisdom. All self-actualization begins with this search. Awareness is consciousness. Developing consciousness is a journey that moves us from the shadows to the light, revealing the true nature of all things. Critical consciousness is the awareness of social, cultural and political forces, and power dynamics that influence our standing in society. Raising consciousness in education is the process of bringing out the natural expression of our self into the world and using it to bring light and nourishment to society.

Individuals and communities that are dealing with chronic stress and adversity may not see the immediate connection between contemplative practices and social justice. This is because mindfulness and meditation have become commercialized and packaged as an individualistic, therapeutic pursuit rather than a pathway for social transformation. The language and lifestyle of yoga and organic living have taken on an air of elitism. For many, holistic practices appear Anglicized, passive and privileged. This is merely a distraction. Contemplative practices are universal. They have always been a powerful force for indigenous, non-Anglo and oppressed people. Contemplation is a deeply spiritual practice essential for self-determination, resilience, freedom and unity.

In 1994, bell hooks wrote about an engaged pedagogy that emphasized a union of mind, body and spirit, and the inner life of teachers and students, connecting learning to life experiences and empowerment. Professors Elisa Facio and Irene Lara, who studied spirituality and activism in Chicana, Latina and indigenous women's lives, wrote a book called *Fleshing the Spirit*, where they share examples of how many of these women rely on the mind-body-spirit relationship to decolonize their minds, find liberation and engage in sacred activism. Laura I. Rendón, Professor Emerita at the University of Texas-San Antonio and writer of *Sentipensante (Sensing/Thinking) Pedagogy: Educating for Wholeness, Social Justice and Liberation*, shares her vision for contemplative education that recognizes cultural patterns of oppression and incorporates a theoretical lens of social justice. As we learn about these diverse perspectives, it becomes easier to embrace contemplation as an inclusive practice that leads to a deeper commitment to social justice.

In his book *The Mindful Brain*, psychiatrist Daniel Siegel points out that mindful awareness is the gateway to accessing more abstract expressions of the brain and human experience. By putting the top-down automatic process of the brain on hold, we free up an abundance of energy that can be used to relieve suffering; discover new perspectives; and cultivate patience, generosity, love and acceptance. By developing the capacity of the mind, we improve our human nature, which is the pathway to inner-peace and conscious social action.

In my first book, *Teacher Agency for Equity: A Framework for Conscientious Engagement*, I posit that the problems we face in society are deeply embedded in our practice—in our language, our norms, our structures and our systems. In order to develop authenticity and agency for change, we need to take on a stance of mindful inquiry and practice new learning models that will lead to equitable practices in schools as well as social transformation. The framework for conscientious engagement centers on three generative practices: Authentic Presence, Freedom and Emergence. Authentic Presence is the integration of the mind, body and spirit in order to inspire and communicate purpose. It involves caring for and aligning our whole self so that we experience well-being and usefulness. Freedom is about adaptability and choosing when to engage or disengage with people (or situations) in order to move into alignment with one's authentic self. This involves an understanding of relationships; power dynamics; and how social, cultural and political factors influence how we see the world and how we behave. The practice of Emergence refers to channeling energy in ways that enable the integration of new ideas for equity. Emergence involves raising consciousness of our interdependence and how we metabolize energy.

In this book, *Mindful Practice for Social Justice: A Guide for Educators and Professional Learning Communities*, I offer individuals and groups a method, strategies and tools to cultivate these practices and teach them to others. It is a professional learning design organized around the three domains of human experience—the Personal, the Social and the Transpersonal. Learning design is an art and science, like architecture. Architects create buildings and structures; learning designers create spaces and conditions for learning. Otto Scharmer and Peter Senge, senior lecturers at MIT, have written at length about the importance of creating holding spaces for professional learning communities. This is one important aspect of learning design—thinking about space and time for groups to make meaning. Frameworks, tools and techniques to help professional learning communities access, process and sift information, and draw out what is most essential is another important aspect of learning design.

As we consider bringing mindfulness and social justice together, professional learning enters new territory because mindfulness involves the study of individual consciousness, and social justice involves the study of the group and fairness. Consciousness is a self-aware, subjective system that has its own free will and is endowed with spiritual presence. Intersubjective social systems, such as relationships, groups and cultural entities, are not self-aware, do not have a will of their own and do not have the same moral or ethical considerations as the individual.[3] Since the practice of education is both an individual and a social endeavor, we need to think about how these two systems interact and influence learning and human development.

Mindfulness is a training. It is a discipline that quiets the internal chatter of the mind. It moves us into a calm and receptive state so that we can refine our attention and direct the flow of information and energy throughout our system. When we practice mindfulness, we become aware of the contents of our mind. We begin to realize just how much our thoughts are influenced by what is going on in our relationships and society. We see this dynamic play out in movies about athletes. When an athlete is training for a competition, for example, she begins to lose momentum and strength when she thinks about a failed relationship or a traumatic experience.

Social justice is about understanding how certain dynamics in our relationships and society can make us feel powerless, weak, vulnerable, afraid, anxious, stressed and unfocused. It is also about identifying and challenging norms, structures and systems that have been built into our institutions that give privilege and power to some at the expense of others. An example of this is a law that bars women or African Americans from voting.

When we bring mindfulness and social justice together in practice, we are recognizing that our state of mind and personal well-being depend upon the state of mind and personal well-being of everybody else in society, and that peace of mind and peace in society are knowing that our basic human rights are protected by the law. By choosing this approach for your professional learning, you are ensuring that you are in the best position to be of service to others with authenticity and purpose, and that you can leverage your professional practice to challenge unfair dynamics in society that impact the quality of life for us all.

The core questions that drive this method are as follows:

◆ Why should I bring mindfulness and social justice into my practice?
◆ What are the essential knowledge and skills associated with mindfulness and social justice?
◆ How can I prepare myself and support others to apply mindfulness and social justice strategies into their everyday practice?
◆ How can we socialize a new generation of educators to advocate for mindfulness and social justice in education and society?

Organization of the Book

The book is organized around the three domains of human experience—the Personal, the Social and the Transpersonal—each one leading to our target practices: Authentic Presence, Freedom and Emergence. There is a specific order and progression of activities, designed to start from the self, or the core, and move the work outward. Once you have gone through the guide one time in sequence, you can go back and pick and choose what you want to focus your attention on for deeper learning.

Chapter 1 connects you with your power, which, according to Dewey, is the basis for all learning. In this chapter, you will end by completing an initial Self-Assessment to situate yourself within a continuum of the practices. Chapter 2 introduces you to the Three Domains of Peak Learning Experience, and provides an overview of the framework and all of its essential components, including learning outcomes, essential questions, strategies, dispositions and barriers. In this chapter, you will also think about observing power and wholeness in others, and how bias and other factors limit our ability to see the truth in people and situations. Chapters 3–5 follow the same format. Each one starts with an overview of the domain followed by an in-depth look at the four strategies, and activities, reflection questions and application to practice tools. Chapter 6 discusses the importance of building the right team and how we need to change the process for recruiting and hiring talent if we want to innovate our profession.

Whenever we involve contemplative practices, we are referring to direct, nonlinear knowing.[4] Each domain presented in this book folds, blends and influences the others. As you engage in the reading and activities, imagine yourself floating along the Milky Way, taking you up and over. For the exercises to work, they have to be a force, not a checklist. This requires a deliberate insertion of time. Each activity has time built in for contemplation and meditation. This time can be extended as you progress. Paying attention to and modifying how we relate to and experience time is central to this method. Activities may feel slow and awkward at first for those new to mindfulness and meditation.

The activities assigned to each strategy draw from knowledge, experience and concrete observations in the field. Many combine and expand on elements from activities that may feel familiar to you. All new learning draws from prior knowledge. However, there is a distinct way in which the activities are designed, framed and positioned within each domain, as well as within the overall progression of the book. Innovating practice requires that we learn from others, try out and investigate different ways of seeing, doing and being, and that we participate in scholar-practitioner research to move the work forward.

To prepare for the writing of this manual, I concentrated on a handful of books, research articles and texts that you will see cited at the end of each chapter. I learned that when we choose an integrated and transdisciplinary pathway for our professional development, we enhance our ability to make connections across content and modify our language and tone to inspire the widest audience. Regardless of the discipline, we are all in search of purpose and meaning.

Throughout the writing of this manual, I practiced daily meditation, yoga, nature walking, running, dialogue, art, cooking, mothering and bearing witness. I lived a simple life, which is not always easy in fast-paced New York City. In my daily practice of meditation, I discovered the elasticity of time and the temporal nature of all things. This is a power tool for people who experience suffering, adversity, hardship and poverty. When you increase your ability to suspend judgment and alter your perception of time and space, you begin to observe how all thoughts, feelings, emotions, sensations and conditions come and go like the tide. Fear, stress and anxiety cease when you realize that "this too shall pass," and each present moment is a prospect. Meditation is free and accessible to anybody, and it requires very little space. Through the natural resource of the mind and spirit, we have access to vision and new life. Some call this a state of grace. Others call it Nirvana. For me, it feels like love and pure consciousness.

It is our job as Master Teachers and practitioners to transmute volumes of information into spiritual nourishment for others. In the end, that is what we all want and need: to be seen, to be loved and to feel useful. The real work is up to you—how you will take the dynamic ideas off these pages and breathe life into them in your unique context. What is essential is nonmaterial and subtle. Learning on some days will feel like an electrical current. On others, a crack in the window.

Notes

1   First People. American Indian Legends. Retrieved from www. firstpeople.us/FP-Html-Legends/TwoWolves-Cherokee.html

2   Sams, J. and Carson, D. (1988) Medicine Cards: The Discovery of Power through the Ways of Animals. Bear and Company, Santa Fe, New Mexico, p. 97.

3   McIntosh, S. (2007) Integral Consciousness and the Future of Evolution. Paragon House, St. Paul, MN, p. 27.

4   Steel, S. (2013) Contemplation as a Corrective to Technological Education, Canadian Journal of Education, Vol. 36, No. 3, pp. 459–480.

1

You are Either Magical, Or You Are Not

Insight into a child's power furnishes the material and becomes the starting point for all education.[1]

John Dewey

In spite of progress and advancements in technology and science, we feel more uncertain now than ever before. Many of us question whether it is possible to live and work together across cultural and ideological differences peacefully and constructively. Information travels at a rapid speed, and life can feel exhilarating, yet we long to slow down, to discover something deeper. Mostly, we want to feel like our life matters. In many ways, we are ripe for a new way of being, a new model for society. This requires a new education.

Over the last few decades, there has been an outpouring of information and research on how we are evolving as human beings. Important discoveries about human development, cognition and brain functioning are influencing every field. Social scientists have expanded our understanding of the nature of relationships, society and the impact of inequality on our overall well-being, our ability to trust, life expectancy, education performance and social mobility.[2] When we stop to observe what is happening, we see two major trends driving our future. The first is the move toward contemplative practices, and the second is the desire for a more egalitarian society.

Teachers and practitioners have enormous influence, individually and collectively. We have wisdom and practical knowledge about human development, transformation and learning that is often left out of text books. Each of us has an important perspective, a wealth of information, a special talent and purpose. What John Dewey says is true—the natural starting point for education is insight into our power, which also sets the highest expectation for ourselves.

Not long ago, I asked one of my precocious teenage students, "What is your superpower?" She replied, "I don't have a superpower." "Really?" I asked. I could hardly hold back a smile. I knew this girl was a talented poet. "Come on," I pushed, "think about it. What is your power?" When she came up blank again, I asked, "Why didn't you say writing?" "Writing? Writing is not a superpower," she replied matter-of-factly, "writing is easy."

Naturally, we associate power with something out of the ordinary, something supernatural or that requires great effort. We also have a tendency to think power comes from somewhere out there. The truth is, our real source of power comes from the natural resources we are given at birth—our talent, our predispositions, and our innate gifts. Some powers are easy to notice, like Mozart's gift for music. Others take time to surface. Parents can usually spot their child's power very early on.

A superpower is a seed, an innate talent that leads us to experience joy and fulfillment. It can be cultivated and recognized by others with discipline and practice. You can have a natural talent for singing, for example, but if you don't practice and cultivate it, it will never be realized to the level of mastery. When you dedicate your life to cultivating and mastering your natural talent or superpower, you are choosing a life of happiness and satisfaction.

What is Your Power?

Many adults have superpowers that lie dormant. Layers of life experience can pull us away from our greatest resource.

The following questions can help us rediscover or affirm our power:

- ♦ What are you naturally good at?
- ♦ What do you enjoy that gives you a sense of satisfaction?
- ♦ What do you spend time fine-tuning and perfecting?
- ♦ What would improve the world?

When I posed these questions to a group of education practitioners, I got an amazing assortment of answers. Here are a few:

Teacher #1
1. What are you naturally good at? *Helping others*
2. What do you enjoy that gives you a sense of satisfaction? *Teaching my students how to read*
3. What do you spend time fine-tuning and perfecting? *Preparing better lessons using hands-on experiences*
4. What would improve the world? *Having more compassionate people*

Professor
1. What are you naturally good at? *Making complicated concepts easy to understand*
2. What do you enjoy that gives you a sense of satisfaction? *Interacting with students*
3. What do you spend time fine-tuning and perfecting? *Making learning fun*
4. What would improve the world? *Being enthusiastic and passionate*

Consultant/Specialist
1. What are you naturally good at? *Sports*
2. What do you enjoy that gives you a sense of satisfaction? *Teaching mindfulness*
3. What do you spend time fine-tuning and perfecting? *Photography*
4. What would improve the world? *Peace and loving-kindness*

Mentor/Coach

1. What are you naturally good at? *Having deep conversations and thinking about solutions to problems*
2. What do you enjoy that gives you a sense of satisfaction? *Traveling and meeting new people*
3. What do you spend time fine-tuning and perfecting? *Understanding race and other social constructs*
4. What would improve the world? *Learning how to work together across race and difference*

Leader

1. What are you naturally good at? *Listening and being with children*
2. What do you enjoy that gives you a sense of satisfaction? *Helping teachers, parents and students*
3. What do you spend time fine-tuning and perfecting? *Life balance and mental health*
4. What would improve the world? *Inner peace and acceptance of differences*

As you review these answers, you can begin to see how Questions 1 and 2 combine to reveal a Power, and the remaining two questions refer to the "how," which is our *Practice*, and the "why," which is our *Purpose*. Playing around with these questions to come up with a *Power to Purpose* statement helps you align your power to your life's work. Our power increases when we realize its utility. Coming up with a Power to Purpose statement is the first step in understanding how all self-actualization leads to something of value in society.

Consider this framing: *"This is who I am and what I love and this is how I can be useful to the world."*

Here are some example **Power to Purpose** statements from the sample group.

Teacher: I help others engage in reading by creating hands-on experiences so that through reading, they learn compassion and understanding of others.

Professor: I make complicated concepts easy to understand by building relationships with students and making learning fun so that they will experience enthusiasm and passion for life.

Consultant/Specialist: I teach about the importance of mindfulness in sports by displaying and analyzing photographs of athletes interacting with each other in training and on the field

Mentor/Coach: I organize opportunities for people to come together to solve problems and reflect on how we can better work together across race and other differences.

Leader: I listen carefully to children in order to gain insight into how we can create school communities that promote well-being, inner peace and acceptance.

Activity

Power to Purpose

Purpose: *To determine your superpower and articulate a Power to Purpose statement so that learning starts from this premise*

♦ Read the four questions, and contemplate them in silence for 5 min before writing anything down.
  • What are you naturally good at?
  • What do you enjoy that gives you a sense of satisfaction?
  • What do you spend time fine-tuning and perfecting?
  • What would improve the world?
♦ After you write your answers, come up with a Power to Purpose Statement.
  • Question 1 + 2 = Power.
  • Question 3 = The "how" or the Practice.
  • Question 4 = The "why" or the Purpose.
♦ If you are working with a partner, consider exchanging your answers to the four questions, and let your partner come up with a Power to Purpose statement for you.
♦ If you are curious about all the fascinating powers that people have reported having, see the Superpowers list in the Appendix.

Barriers and Limitations to Power

Sometimes, we have difficulty recognizing or valuing our power. This may have to do with social conditioning, judgment, chronic adversity or oppression. If your natural power has not been appreciated, rewarded or cultivated over time, it can fall dormant. All of our interactions in society, starting from birth, influence how we feel about our innate traits, attributes, dispositions and talents. What we consider powerful and worthy is learned from experience and norms prevalent in society.

Thinking about work situations can reveal how we are easily influenced by normative values and beliefs which translate into how we feel about ourselves, our power and worthiness. For example, when I was part of a large education organization, I observed how the employees who were agreeable were the ones who got promoted and celebrated. In contrast, employees who asked lots of questions or who didn't smile as much were overlooked or slighted. There were also privileges bestowed upon those who had political connections and came from money. For those employees who had none of these things and challenged norms or traditional modes of thinking, there was no real sense of belonging or job security.

Some powers are subtle and are revealed in extraordinary contexts. In his book *Schindler's List*, Thomas Keneally tells us the story of when Clara Sternberg loses all hope in Auschwitz. As she looks for a way to throw herself onto the electric fence, an acquaintance tells her, "Don't kill yourself on the fence, Clara. If you do that, you'll never know what happened to you." This was the most powerful of answers to give a woman intending suicide. *Kill yourself, and you'll never find out how the plot ends.*[3] Somehow, this woman was able to use her words to convince Clara to turn around and live. Knowing how to say exactly the right thing at the right time to transform the path of a person's life is a perfect example of a superpower that might be overlooked if we don't pay attention.

Personal Reflection

♦ Think about a time when you might have underestimated or undervalued your power because you were discouraged or distracted by an individual, group or professional situation.
   • What happened? Where you able to reclaim your power? What did you do?
   • How can you make sure you keep your powers at the center of your professional practice?
   • How can we socialize students to value their powers and respect the powers of others?

Getting Started: Initial Self-Assessment

Now that we have established that you are a powerful, purposeful being, you are ready to begin. Your ability to do this work depends on your discipline and commitment to training your mind, modifying behaviors, reflecting on experience and applying new learning to your professional practice. You will learn to pay attention to and activate the three domains of human experience so that you can use your own personal experience as the foundation for creating similar learning conditions for others. The future learning environment is a fluid, dynamic space where master practitioners employ instruction and interaction techniques that provide students with a wide range of transcensory learning modalities so that they can access, explore and practice new learning individually and with peers.

Now is a good time to take a Self-Assessment. The Self-Assessment is a diagnostic tool divided into three parts, each aligned with the three domains. The three domains are Authentic Presence, Freedom and Emergence.

Partaking in a simple Self-Assessment will help you identify where you are at the start of your journey and establish some guidelines to track your progress.

You can find the Self-Assessment on the next three pages. When you are finished, keep your answers close as you will refer back to them throughout the book.

Self-Assessment Part 1. Authentic Presence

Directions: Read across each row, and circle the statement that best describes you.

DOMAIN 1 Authentic Presence Self-Assessment Tool

	Level 1	Level 2	Level 3	Level 4
1.	I don't engage in contemplative practices or meditation	I have tried a contemplative practice or meditation to calm my mind	I practice contemplation or meditation regularly to calm my mind and to raise consciousness	I practice contemplation or meditation regularly to calm my mind, raise consciousness and to gain insight into how I can better the world through my practice
2.	I don't engage in physical activity and/or practice yoga	I occasionally engage in physical activity and/or practice yoga	I regularly engage in physical activity and/or practice yoga	I regularly engage in physical activity and practice yoga, and I apply insights from these activities to my practice
3.	I have little knowledge of my identity and culture	I am exploring my identity and culture but don't feel confident communicating about these topics	I have knowledge of my identity and culture, and feel confident communicating on these topics	I have knowledge about my identity and culture, and I feel confident communicating on these topics and explaining how these factors influence my practice
4.	I do not see how acting or performance techniques apply to my practice	I see how acting or performance techniques apply to my practice but I don't put much effort in this area	I regularly use acting or performance techniques in my practice in order to influence and inspire others	I regularly use acting and performance techniques in my practice in order to influence and inspire others on topics related to social justice

Self-Assessment Part 2. Freedom

Directions: Read across each row, and circle the statement that best describes you.

DOMAIN 2 Freedom Self-Assessment Tool

	Level 1	Level 2	Level 3	Level 4
1.	I have never engaged in an intergroup dialogue	I have engaged in one intergroup dialogue	I engage in intergroup dialogues, and I am aware of patterns in how norms, systems, policies and programs impact various populations	I engage and facilitate intergroup dialogues to help others become aware of how systems, policies and programs have impacted various populations
2.	I do not participate in rituals or ceremonies at work	I participate in one or two rituals or ceremonies at work	I participate in rituals and ceremonies at work, and I am aware of how they communicate values and build community	I participate in rituals and ceremonies at work, and I feel confident disengaging when they don't align with my values in a way that could lead to learning and transformation
3.	I don't use technology and the internet in my practice	I use technology and the internet in my practice to communicate and explore learning opportunities	I rely on technology and the internet in my practice to communicate, explore learning opportunities and network	I balance my use of technology and the internet with other modes of communication in order to respond thoughtfully to each person and situation
4.	I don't think much about adversity, suffering and human rights issues	I think about adversity, suffering and human rights issues	I think about adversity, suffering and human rights issues, and reflect on how these issues impact my practice	I think about and learn from adversity, suffering and human rights issues, individually and with colleagues, in order to improve our practice for social justice

Self-Assessment Part 3. Emergence

Directions: Read across each row, and circle the statement that best describes you.

DOMAIN 3   Emergence Self-Assessment Tool

	Level 1	Level 2	Level 3	Level 4
1.	I have not engaged in image-based explorations related to my practice	I have engaged in image-based explorations related to my practice, but I am not sure of their impact	I have engaged in image-based explorations related to my practice and understand how they cultivate creativity	I engage in image-based explorations related to my practice to cultivate creativity and to support envisioning and problem-solving for social justice
2.	I am not familiar with wisdom traditions nor do I engage in philosophical conversations	I have explored some wisdom traditions and have engaged in philosophical conversations, but not with colleagues	I have explored wisdom traditions and have engaged in philosophical conversations with colleagues, but I am not sure how to apply to my practice	I explore wisdom traditions and engage in philosophical conversations with colleagues and discuss how we can apply insights to our practice for social justice
3.	I have not engaged in an inquiry cycle	I have engaged in an inquiry cycle on a topic related to my practice	I engage in inquiry cycles on topics related to my practice and social justice	I engage in shared mindful inquiry cycles with colleagues on topics related to our practice and social justice
4.	I do not think about energy and power dynamics	I have thought about energy and power dynamics, but I am not sure how they play out in my practice	I understand how energy and power dynamics play out in my practice, but I am not sure how to intervene in ways that would improve the situation	I can assess energy and power dynamics, and I can intervene in ways that realize potential and maximize performance with equity in mind

Notes

1 Dewey, J. (1929) My Pedagogical Creed, *Journal of the National Education Association,* Vol. 18, No. 9, pp. 291–295.
2 Wilkinson, R. and Pickett, K. (2010) *The Spirit Level, Why Greater Equality Makes Societies Stronger.* Bloomsbury Press, New York & London, p. 19.
3 Keneally, T. (1993) *Schindler's List, Touchtone Edition.* Simon and Schuster, New York, p. 321.

2

Three Domains for Peak Learning Experience

What we need is protected time and space to do the type of raising consciousness for equity work needed that will lead us to new thinking and new ways of doing.[1]

The new education paradigm is about human experience. Human experience activates mind-body-spirit to move us beyond the material plane so that we can realize potential and transform society into one that is more just and loving. The purpose of all learning is to raise consciousness, to develop the capacity to work effectively together across differences and to improve our quality of life. Learning organizations of the future will be centers where Master Teachers and students study consciousness and practice manifesting ideas into reality.

Human potential is both intrinsic and relational. Interactions in the environment lead to reciprocal transformation, which strengthens individual and collective agency. Implicit in the new paradigm is the notion that human beings are at a critical point in evolution. We know that thought and belief, which are nonmaterial and subtle, impact brain functioning, our physical health and well-being, and our ability to function effectively in society. We also know that equitable systems improve our individual well-being and the quality of life for everybody.[2]

In this work, you are in the position of a Master Teacher. A Master Teacher is conscious of our basic goodness, is disciplined and knowledgeable about the development of potential and recognizes that integral to teaching is shepherding others through change and adaptability. As discussed in the previous chapter, the starting point for all education is the recognition of personal power and putting our power to purpose—in other words, to become useful in society and assist in human evolution. When we shepherd others through and into change, we are teaching human beings how to adapt to any situation without losing power and purpose, so that we can work together to advance civilization. This is the work of a master.

The theory of action is guiding students through Peak Learning Experience and human interactions that lead to Personal Awareness and Self-Mastery, Social Awareness and Adaptability, Transpersonal Awareness and Agency. When we teach and learn in this way, we discover that all human experience is about appreciating our fundamental goodness, achieving happiness and using our power to bring happiness and well-being to others.

Peak Learning Experience is when we become aware of or conscious of our infinite potential and capability. It is the realization that all things are possible and that we are part of a creative universe in which we have the power to determine the shape and content of our lives.

Human beings are multisensory and transcensory beings. We have the ability to see ourselves and the world differently, for goodness, for power and potential and for wholeness. Scientists believe that parts of our brain are designed to expand our vision and to help us see differently, holistically. Wisdom and spiritual traditions refer to a sixth sense or divine intelligence. Some call it a field of consciousness. Artists speak of a somewhat altered state of awareness that can be entered, while drawing for example. They describe it as feeling alert and aware yet relaxed and free from anxiety, experiencing a pleasurable, almost mystical activation of the mind.[3] This mystical activation of the mind is the gateway to higher-order thinking skills, such as problem-solving and decision-making. Drawing, like all art creation, is one example of contemplative practice. Another is meditation. These are entry points for your beginning understanding of Peak Learning Experience.

When we bring mindfulness and social justice together in practice, we are exploring these dynamic aspects of human experience and learning how to apply them to our work in education. This means that we will be engaging in contemplative practices and activities that help us to access different parts of our brain. We know that different tasks activate specific brain regions and that experiences such as stress can affect brain functioning and result in increased anxiety or aggression, or impair decision-making and judgment.[4] Our goal is to create experience that will lead to greater emotional stability and decreased anxiety, more effective thinking and planning, and higher moral reasoning. As we experience these things, we will reflect on that experience and draw out important knowledge and skills that we can use in our work teaching and supporting others.

As mentioned earlier, learning is organized into three domains—the Personal, the Social and the Transpersonal. Each domain responds to three generative practices: Authentic Presence, Freedom and Emergence (Figure 2.1).

- ♦ **Authentic Presence**: Personal Awareness and Self-Mastery;
- ♦ **Freedom**: Social Awareness and Adaptability;
- ♦ **Emergence**: Transpersonal Awareness and Agency.

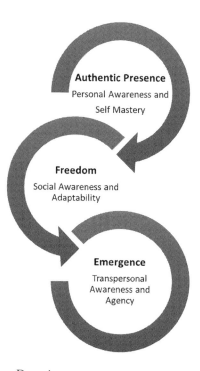

Authentic Presence
Personal Awareness and
Self Mastery

Freedom
Social Awareness and
Adaptability

Emergence
Transpersonal
Awareness and
Agency

FIGURE 2.1   The Three Domains.

In the following page, you will find the framework and the key components. Take a moment now to review the chart. What do you notice? In the following pages, you will find an overview and a brief description of each component.

Three Domains for Peak Learning Experience Framework

Domains	Authentic Presence (Inner Work)	Freedom (Outer Work)	Emergence (Spirit /Soul Work)
Learning Outcomes	Personal Awareness and Self-Mastery	Social Awareness and Adaptability	Transpersonal Awareness and Agency
Essential Questions	Who am I? Who are we?	How do I behave with others? How do we behave and interact with each other?	What is my purpose? What is our purpose?
Strategies	1. Contemplation and Meditation 2. Movement and Yoga 3. Identity and Culture Study 4. Acting and Performance	1. Intergroup Dialogue 2. Rituals and Ceremony 3. Balanced Technology 4. Bearing Witness	1. Envisioning and Imagination 2. Wisdom Traditions and Philosophy 3. Shared Mindful Inquiry 4. Channeling Energy
Dispositions	Reflective Focused Self-Assured Inspiring	Trustworthy Inclusive Responsive Compassionate	Creative Wise Curious Powerful
Barriers	Impatience Stress Hypocrisy Fear	Guilt Isolation Rigidity Shame	Cynicism Egotism Complacency Fatigue

Overview of Authentic Presence

All human beings are made up of mind, body and spirit, and therefore have access to a creative, divine intelligence. Authentic Presence is the capacity to integrate the mind, body and spirit in order to inspire and communicate purpose. Personal Awareness and Self-Mastery lead to Authentic Presence. It involves familiarizing ourselves with the function of the mind, body and spirit, and learning how to care for and align them so that we experience well-being and utility in the world.

Learning Outcomes and Essential Questions

Who am I? Who are We? are the driving questions behind Authentic Presence. We learn about individuality, but we also learn non-duality. We are individuals, but we are also "part of" a greater whole. For this reason, we can track and study patterns in human experience, such as the experience of being an infant and being a teenager or growing old. Likewise, most individuals identify with a culture, language or ethnicity. Personal Awareness and Self-Mastery is recognizing and appreciating the "I" and understanding how we are also part of a "We."

Strategies

A strategy is an approach, method or technique used to reach our goal. For Authentic Presence, the four strategies are **Contemplation and Meditation, Movement and Yoga, Identity and Culture Study, Acting and Performance.**

Dispositions

Dispositions refer to a state of being and mind-set. The dispositions associated with Authentic Presence are **Reflective, Focused, Self-Assured and Inspiring.**

Barriers

Anticipating difficulties that might arise keeps us vigilant and provides us with entry points for personal reflection and improvement. The barriers associated with Authentic Presence are **Impatience, Stress, Hypocrisy and Fear.**

Overview of Freedom

We are entangled with some people more than others, and these relationships impact how we behave in the world. Freedom is about choosing to engage or disengage with people (or a situation) in order to move into alignment with one's authentic self. Social Awareness and Adaptability are required for Freedom. They entail an understanding of the function of relationships and society, and how social, cultural and political factors influence how we see the world and how we behave. Freedom is our ability to situate ourselves within the context of society and adapt to situations in order to work with others toward a common goal while maintaining authenticity and purpose.

Targets

How do I behave with others? How do we behave and interact with each other? We are responsible for our own behavior, but we are also part of a community. We engage at work, in public, in rituals and in ceremonies that give us a sense of belonging and community, and through these structures, we express ourselves, love others and pass down knowledge to future generations. Our survival depends on our ability to adapt our behavior to a wide range of situations and conditions. We learn that our well-being is dependent on the well-being of everybody else.

Strategies

A strategy is an approach, method or technique used to reach our goal. There are four strategies associated with each domain. For Freedom, the four strategies are **Intergroup Dialogue, Rituals and Ceremonies, Balanced Technology and Bearing Witness**.

Dispositions

Dispositions refer to habits, a state of being and a mind-set. For Freedom, the dispositions are **Trustworthy, Inclusive, Responsive, Compassionate**.

Barriers

Anticipating difficulties that might arise keeps us vigilant and provides us with entry points for personal reflection and improvement. The barriers associated with Freedom are **Guilt, Isolation, Rigidity, Shame**.

Overview of Emergence

Through human effort, we imagine and build a better world. Emergence is the capacity to channel human energy in ways that enable the integration of new ideas. All ideas that have value lead to improving the quality of life for everybody. Transpersonal Awareness and Agency are required for Emergence. This involves understanding that all human experience extends beyond the material world and involves energy. Envisioning new realities and learning how to channel individual and collective energy toward a common goal is central to Emergence.

Targets

What is my purpose? What is our purpose? Human beings are naturally born with curiosity and the desire to explore the meaning of life. In all fields, whether science or religion, we are searching for answers to the nature of our existence. We learn how all knowledge and traditions, and advancements in the sciences converge around universal wisdom that teaches us consciousness and how we can assist in human evolution.

Strategies

A strategy is an approach, method or technique used to reach our goal. The strategies that lead to Emergence are **Envisioning and Imagination, Wisdom Traditions and Philosophy, Shared Mindful Inquiry, Channeling Energy**.

Dispositions

Dispositions refer to a state of being and mind-set. For Emergence, the dispositions are **Creative, Wise, Curious, Powerful**.

Barriers

Anticipating difficulties that might arise keeps us vigilant and provides us with entry points for personal reflection and improvement. The barriers associated with Emergence are **Cynicism, Egotism, Complacency, Fatigue**.

Becoming Aware of Human Experience

In education, we emphasize learning and communication through language and reason. There is a focus on left side of the brain thinking, which specializes in linguistics, linearity, logic and literal thinking.[5] This ends up dominating how we talk about our experience in the world. We spend much less time thinking about how we communicate with our bodies, and rarely do we discuss the subtle language of the spirit. This is because the spirit communicates in nuanced and complex ways, including through intuition, dreams, imagination, art, music and energy. When we talk about getting a vibe from somebody, for example, we are talking about the energy that passes between people in the field of space and time. All three domains—mind, body and spirit—act out and communicate in the world continuously and simultaneously and influence how we learn.

In order for us to become aware of human experience and to see the whole truth of a person or situation, we can practice *transcensory perception*. Transcendence is *moving beyond* just the physical plane or *rising above* the limitations of the physical world. Transcensory perception is opening the door to a "sixth sense," so to speak, which involves the third domain associated with Transpersonal Awareness. Transcensory perception is being open and receptive to the idea that in order for us to capture human experience, we must involve insight, wisdom and intuition, all of which are subtle and nuanced, and refined over time by attention. For many practitioners trained in the sciences, this is taboo. We have been trained to believe that the observer is separate, independent and objective. Involving intuition, wisdom and insight does not mean that we are not rigorous or critical, or that we do not test the truth. It just means that we recognize that the observer contributes to what is being observed through a refined attention, in other words, our state of mind or consciousness.

Transcensory observation is a form of *meditative observation*, and we can practice it by applying three techniques: Setting Intention, Bearing Witness and Suspending Judgment.

Transcensory Observation Techniques

◆ **Setting Intention**: An intention directs your attention and energy to an outcome. The outcome is typically a disposition, virtue or state of being. Sometimes we want to connect an intention to a particular problem you want to solve, such as thinking about how to resolve a conflict with a student, boss or colleague. An intention of this nature would take the form of a statement. For example, *I'm looking for insight into how to best respond to my boss tomorrow.*

◆ **Bearing Witness**: To acknowledge that human experience is real and true, that all experience is, in one way or another, shared human phenomena. Positioning ourselves outside experience, independent of it, as if the experience has nothing to do with us, creates a barrier to seeing truth and responding with empathy. Bearing witness involves being with, blending into, becoming a part of experience so that the image of the person suffering or experiencing joy blends with your own image.

◆ **Suspending Judgment**: Suspending judgment requires us to notice with awareness and openness without analyzing, evaluating, comparing, creating a hierarchy or drawing conclusions.

Training for a Master Teacher involves becoming aware of human experience through refined attention and opening our mind and heart to everyday, ordinary experience. Refined attention requires wisdom and learning to trust our intuition. Wisdom comes from experience and learning from sacred knowledge passed down from generation to generation. Intuition is our ability to know or understand something without any logic or reasoning. All human beings have intuition. Written work examining intuition goes way back to the Aztec, Babylonian, Greek, Hebraic and Chinese cultures as well as in the Hindu and Buddhist thought. Intuition has been the topic of great exploration and has been included in the work of Plato and Aristotle. Carl Jung proposed that intuition was one of the four ways that human beings processed the world. Everybody has intuition; however, we may have a more or less developed awareness of it.[6]

Activities

1. Intuitive Mime

Purpose: To learn how to trust our intuition

Overview: Two people mirror each other's behavior and reflect on the experience

- ◆ You will need a partner, room enough to move around and a timer.
- ◆ Stand facing your partner.
- ◆ Set the Intention: *Intuitive*.
  - An intention directs your attention and energy to an outcome. The outcome is typically a disposition, virtue or state of being.
  - Sometimes, we connect an intention to a particular problem that we want to solve, such as how to resolve a conflict with a student, boss or colleague. An intention of this nature would take the form of a statement such as "Using my intuition in order to understand why a student is behaving in that way."
- ◆ Move yourselves into exactly the same position, mirroring each other. Freeze in the mirrored position. Set the timer for 3 min.
  - Breathe.
  - Try not to laugh or change facial expression.
  - Stand in quiet observation of the other.
- ◆ When the timer goes off, set the timer again for 10 min.
- ◆ Get into another frozen position. This time, one person should start to move spontaneously and gradually. The other person should follow the movements as if they were the mirror image while keeping eye contact.
  - Keep moving slowly for the duration of the time.
  - Pause and give each person the chance to lead the next move.
  - Each move should be free and natural, using the whole body.

- ◆ Reflect individually in writing or discuss your partner. Set the timer for 7 min.
  - • How did it feel mirroring your partner's moves?
  - • How did you know when and in which direction to move?
  - • Did the mirroring get easier as you went along?
  - • What did you learn about yourself?
  - • What did you observe about your partner?

2. SIFT[7] Observation (Sensations, Images, Feelings, Thoughts)

Purpose: To become aware of the contents of your mind during an observation

Overview: Participants conduct an observation and take notes about what they see using a sifting protocol

- ◆ You will need paper, a pencil and a timer.
- ◆ Choose a social situation to observe.
  - • You can observe any social activity in which more than one person is involved.
  - • Consider a busy public space, such as a park, shopping mall, museum, busy street corner, recess at a school, cafeteria or hospital lobby.
- ◆ To prepare, divide your page into quadrants.
  - • Label: Sensations, Images, Feelings, Thoughts.
- ◆ Pre-Observation. Observe without writing. Set the timer for 5 min.
  - • Just breathe and relax.
  - • Bring to mind *Transcensory Observation Techniques*.
- ◆ Observe for Sensations, Images, Feelings, Thoughts. Set the timer for 15 min.
  - • Write down your observations into the appropriate boxes.
    - ◆ **Sensations:** Reactions associated with the body, such as hunger, cold, hot, numb;
    - ◆ **Feelings:** Emotions such as sad, excited, apathetic, bored;
    - ◆ **Images:** Everything you capture with your eyes, visuals;
    - ◆ **Thoughts:** Ideas, opinions, narratives in the mind.

- ◆ Afterward, individually reflect on your observation notes. Set the timer for 5 min.
- ◆ Individually write or discuss with a partner:
  - How would you describe this experience?
  - What was challenging or surprising about the SIFT protocol?
  - Are you able to make connections between images and feelings? How about between thoughts and sensations?
  - What insights surfaced?

Implicit Bias Revisited

Implicit bias is a result of the automatic processes of the brain that sort, categorize and detect patterns in information, and make associations with emotional responses. Depending on what images and information you are exposed to on a regular basis, your brain makes associations. For example, if you watch television every day, and live in the United States, over time you are likely to associate thin, blonde females with desirability and low intelligence and Muslim men with anger and terrorism. Associations are not true; instead, they are determined patterns or constructed images developed over years of social conditioning. Cultural contexts, upbringing, dominant political narratives, media and education are all influences that impact our perception of human beings and situations.

Implicit bias is similar to stereotyping, in that it involves making generalizations; however, implicit bias specifically refers to when we unconsciously attach negative or positive emotional responses to people or situations. We learn through our associations what is good or bad, what is threatening or safe. If we perceive a person or situation to be good for us, we move in that direction. Conversely, if we perceive a threat, we reject it. When we act on the automatic processes of the brain, we are acting without consciousness which can be harmful to others.

It is natural for the brain to make associations, to process and interpret information. By training the mind, we can put the automatic processes on hold, calm our thoughts and refine our attention so that we can determine right action. A Master

Teacher knows not to rely solely on the automatic processes of our brain because the brain does not take into account the totality of human experience, our human vulnerabilities and our susceptibility to bias.

Practicing transcensory observation can help mitigate bias. We do this practice alone and work with others to calibrate our observation findings. Calibrating is a tuning protocol that involves two people observing the same person or situation with the same intention and comparing observation data. Sharing data, communicating what we observe and learning how others perceive the same person or situation increases awareness, and even more so when we are calibrating with an individual from a different background.

Notes

1   Rios, R. (2017) *Teacher Agency for Equity: A Framework for Conscientious Engagement*. Routledge, New York, p. 54.

2   Wilkinson, R. and Pickett, K. (2010) *The Spirit Level, Why Greater Equality Makes Societies Stronger*. Bloomsbury Press, New York & London, p. 33.

3   Edwards, B. (1999) *Drawing on the Right Side of the Brain*. Penguin Putnam, New York.

4   Travis, F. (2009) Brain Functioning as the Ground for Spiritual Experiences and Ethical Behavior, *The FBI Law Enforcement Bulletin*, Vol. 78.

5   Siegel, D. (2007) *The Mindful Brain, Mind Your Brain*. W. W. Norton & Company Inc., New York & London, pp. 45–46.

6   Franquemont, S. (2009) Retrieved from www.intuitionworks.com/ history.htm

7   Siegel, D. (2007) *The Mindful Brain, Mind Your Brain*. W. W. Norton & Company Inc., New York & London, p. 19.

3

Authentic Presence

Personal Awareness and Self-Mastery

Consciousness has the power to look upon thought with love, compassion and forgiveness, all of which frees ourselves from thought completely.[1]

Human beings are made up of mind, body and spirit, and have access to a creative, divine intelligence. Authentic Presence is the capacity to integrate the mind, body and spirit in order to inspire and communicate purpose. Personal Awareness and Self-Mastery lead to Authentic Presence. This involves knowing how the mind, body and spirit function so that you can activate them and bring your whole self into the education space with grace and confidence.

In this chapter, we explore four strategies and techniques that lead to Authentic Presence. We will engage in activities, reflect on experience and think about how we can apply Authentic Presence to our practice.

The following are dispositions and barriers associated with Authentic Presence. It is important to recognize and anticipate them. At the end of each strategy, you will be prompted to think about a disposition to help you process your learning. At the end of the chapter, you will have the opportunity to synthesize your experience, consider barriers and learn how to apply to practice.

Dispositions

Reflective: Taking the time to carefully consider and examine experience; being open and willing to slow down, outwardly and inwardly, in order to gain insight and understanding;

Focused: Being able to minimize distractions and pay attention through concentration;

Self-Assured: Having an appreciation of your unique character, identity and culture; confident in your abilities;

Inspiring: Being able to breathe new life into; having the ability to encourage, motivate, stimulate, move a person to new action.

Barriers

Impatience: The experience of disappointment, nervousness and anxiety when a situation or experience takes longer than desired or anticipated.

Stress: An uncomfortable emotional experience produced by a real or perceived threat resulting in physiological and behavioral changes.

Hypocrisy: Behavior that contradicts professed beliefs, principles or values.

Fear: An unpleasant emotion caused by the belief that a person or situation is dangerous and will cause pain or suffering.

Strategy 1. Contemplation and Meditation

> Raising our consciousness is a pathway and a real source of energy that enables human beings to take on miraculous feats.[2]

On a blistery cold day, I ventured into a warm and beautiful meditation center in New York City. I had been practicing meditation at home, and wanted to experience what it was like to meditate in a public space, with a live teacher. I learned two important lessons from that visit. First, architecture and space impact our state of mind and receptivity to new experience. Second, meditating in a group with the guidance of a teacher has important benefits.

The center had an open design, with tall windows and hidden sky lights where natural light seeped in. The concrete clutter and chaos of the Manhattan street seemed far off in the distance. The architecture was characterized by long, uninterrupted lines, high ceilings and plenty of space to walk around. It felt expansive and within my reach simultaneously. The lecture and meditation took place in a large, carpeted room with cubbies for our shoes. The teacher entered promptly following a soft chime. He wore simple, well-fitted clothing and carried a book. He took his place on a medium-sized, raised platform. He sat comfortably but dignified with a tall, straight back and legs crossed. His voice was soothing and his pacing slow. He interjected personal stories making the material relatable. He explained the type of meditation we were about to practice and I felt at ease, curious and safe. When we meditated together, I felt like we were transmitting energy to one another. It was like being at Yankee Stadium as a child and getting swept up by the wave.

Our preparation begins here, with these understandings. All of our work starts and emerges from contemplation. We will take insights that surface from contemplative practice and apply them to our professional development, how we interact in social situations and how we think about guiding and supporting students.

Contemplative practices cultivate awareness by turning one's attention inward. There are many contemplative practices, and the primary one is meditation. Others include deep listening, chanting, yoga, nature observation, self-inquiry, self-reflection, art creation, journaling, hiking, jogging, silence retreat and so on. There is a difference between hiking and jogging "mindlessly" versus "mindfully." If we are daydreaming about what we will be doing that night or what happened yesterday, then we are not engaging in a contemplative practice. Contemplative practice involves being aware, each moment, of what we are doing as we are doing it.[3]

Typically, we are drawn to a contemplative practice that feels natural but it is a good idea to explore many. Each one gives you different insights into yourself and human experience. I started with contemplative journaling because I enjoy writing but when I tried yoga, I discovered my tolerance for discomfort and discipline. I learned about breathing and how my breathing impacts my ability to be flexible. These lessons were important to my understanding of productive struggle: a concept we apply to our work in the classroom.

In his book, *The Mindful Brain*, psychiatrist Daniel Siegel describes the activities of the mind as Sensations, Images, Feelings and Thoughts (SIFT). In the previous chapter, we were introduced to SIFT when we practiced transcensory observation. Through contemplative practice, we experience the process of discernment, where we become aware that our mind's activities are not the totality of who we are. It allows us to recognize and disassociate ourselves from the automatic narratives in the brain so we are not ensnarled or paralyzed by an internal battle between thoughts, sensations, feelings, images and what we think "ought to be." When we let go of our attachment or overidentification with the activities of the brain, we free up an abundance of energy. For a Master Teacher in training, contemplative practice is essential because the mirror properties of the brain suggest that how we arrive as teachers ourselves will directly activate these states in the student.[4]

The three goals of contemplative practices and meditation are as follows: (1) learning from firsthand experience, (2) expanding perception of time and (3) focusing on an intention, even if the intention is to be present.[5]

Learning from Firsthand Experience

In science we understand the world and build knowledge by analyzing external phenomena using instruments and experimentation to draw conclusions. Science assumes that data being analyzed within an experiment are independent of the preconceptions, perceptions and experience of the scientist.[6] In contrast, contemplative investigation is understanding the world and building knowledge by developing refined attention, which is then used in the examination of inner experience. The conclusions drawn from contemplative investigation are typically referred to as insights and the underlying assumption is one of interdependence and non-duality. There is no separation between the self and others, between the observer and what is being observed.

Expanding Perception of Time

The realization that we can alter our perception of time is encouraging. We never feel we have enough time in education. Conversely, when we are faced with challenging circumstances, time feels like an eternity. Our perception of time wields power over how we feel and how we approach our practice. Time can make the difference between success or failure in the real world. For this reason, teachers go back and forth between telling students to take their time, when there is something important at stake and to hurry up in order to meet a deadline. As we get older, we experience zenosyne, the feeling that time keeps getting faster and faster. It is a built-in mechanism to remind us that wisdom comes from learning how to appreciate time and to live in the moment.

We can explore the notion of time and our perception of it by thinking about the following idioms and expressions. What do they mean? What value or belief do they communicate?

- No time like the present;
- Stop killing time;
- Behind the times;
- Time is money;
- Delayed gratification;
- Sense of urgency;
- Time flies;
- Doing time.

Culture and Perception of Time

There is an association between our perception of time and culture. When I worked in the Middle East with a predominantly American team, for example, it appeared that everything was taking too long. We were forced to examine our attitudes related to time, especially when thinking about the topic of effective leadership and management. In our examination of the issues, we discovered cultural bias in our approach and curriculum. Western culture tends to view time as linear, with a definitive beginning and end; time is viewed as limited in supply, so we structure our lives accordingly. In other cultures, time is perceived as cyclical and endless. More importance is placed on doing things right and maintaining harmony.[7] It is our attitude and our perception about time that causes frustration, not time itself. Once we learn this lesson, we are better able to adapt ourselves and respond wisely to the situation.

Equity and Perception of Time

Time can raise concerns about values, fairness and equity. Making information accessible and relevant to all students and individualizing instruction require time. How much time we have for preparation, how much time we allocate to individual students and how much time we assign to an activity—all of these decisions matter and communicate what we value. Often, these decisions feel imposed upon us by systems and our own education that reflect normative perceptions of time. An example of this is tardiness. If we feel contempt or disdain for a student because we associate his tardiness with how much he values his education, his health or what have you, we are not open to exploring all the possible reasons for tardiness that have nothing to do with a person's integrity or motivation.

Contemplative practices, and meditation in particular, force us to engage with time differently. It alters our perception, teaches time elasticity and the temporal nature of all things. Have you heard of the phrase, a watched pot never boils? When we understand how time is a subjective experience and relative to our context, we can choose how to engage with it in our lives and in our practice; we can also advocate for systems and structures that are more elastic and responsive. A student, parent or client who is suffering, unemployed or hungry, for example, will have a very different perception of time and a greater sense of urgency as compared to someone who is healthy, employed and well-fed.

Focus

When we learn to focus our attention on an intention, even if the intention is being present, we reduce stress and anxiety, and clear our mind from the clutter that distracts us from our purpose.

The more we learn to train our mind to concentrate and direct our thoughts, the more we experience agency because we are positioning ourselves in the driver's seat. One of the best ways to train the mind and learn how to focus attention is through the practice of meditation.

Meditation

Meditation is the gateway to altered states of consciousness and freedom. (See Figure 3.1) It is the experience of the limitless nature of the mind when it ceases to be dominated by the usual mental chatter. If the mind is continually clouded by thoughts, we are never able to experience it in and of itself. When we experience the mind in and of itself, we find our true nature that is calm and serene.[8] When we experience a calm mind, we experience liberation from all the thoughts, emotions and life circumstances that weigh us down. Meditation is the attainment of lightness of being. It is like transforming ourselves into an eagle. Have you ever watched an eagle? It leaps off a tree or mountain and starts its flight. Higher and higher it goes until it soars effortlessly, without needing to flap its wings. What does the eagle see from way up there? Once we are in this high, open space, we can see things from a distance. Our perspective has changed; while gliding, we observe. From this vantage point, we can choose to

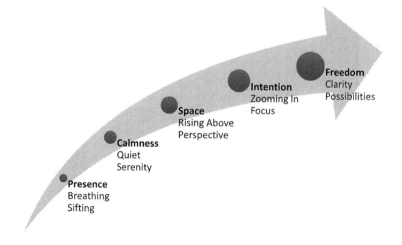

FIGURE 3.1 Meditation and Freedom.

zoom in and fly down, to any point. Have you ever watched an eagle dive down from an enormous height in seconds and swoop in on a target without losing balance? This is pure freedom and power. This is how we gain awareness and, at the same time, deep insight.

Meditation takes time and practice like any discipline. At the beginning, it is normal to feel discouraged. Stick with it and investigate strategies to support your meditation practice. Some people like to start with a meditation tape, a teacher guide or work with a group. There are countless books on the topic of meditation. Here are a few basics:

1. Sit in a comfortable position with your back straight and tall. It can be on the floor, a chair or pillow. Most people cross their legs. Do not slouch, relax your shoulders.
2. Set a timer. Start for shorter intervals such as 5 min, then increase gradually.
3. Let your hands rest on your knees, palms up. Alternatively, you can hold your hands together and rest them in the center of your lap. Some people like touching the tips of their fingers together creating a triangle or another shape. Think of your arms and hands as an energy conduit.
4. Breathe deeply paying attention to how the air flows in and out of your nostrils. Fill up your lungs completely before exhaling. After a few intervals of deep breathing, begin to breathe naturally, keeping your attention on the feeling of air moving in and out your nose and traveling throughout your body.
5. When a thought enters your mind, distracting you from your breath, tell it to move on gently. Once the mind is calm and free of thought, you can concentrate on an intention, even if the intention is to be present. Don't fight yourself. Be gentle. Clearing the mind and entering subtle awareness takes practice.
6. You may consider incense or light, instrumental music. Avoid music that is fast or with lyrics.

Activities

1. Quotes, Sayings or Mantra Meditation

Purpose: To consider how meditation impacts our thinking about a topic

Overview: Participants read a quote, engage in a short meditation and share insights

- ◆ You will need a quote and a timer.
  - • For this activity, we are going to use a quote by Arundhati Roy from her novel *The God of Small Things*.
  - • "Change is one thing. Acceptance is another."[9]
  - • You should begin to collect quotes, sayings and mantras related to topics of human significance and social justice.
  - • Keep them written on index cards in a box to use for your contemplation practice.
  - • Choose quotes, sayings or mantras that reflect a wide range of cultures and identities.
- ◆ Get into a comfortable spot on the floor, on a chair or on a sofa. Cross your legs, straighten your back.
- ◆ Set the Intention: Insight.
  - • An intention directs your attention and energy to an outcome. The outcome is typically a disposition, virtue or state of being.
  - • Sometimes, we connect an intention to a particular problem we want to solve, such as how to resolve a conflict with a student, boss or colleague. An intention of this nature would take the form of a statement such as "Gaining insight in order to better understand how to support _____."
- ◆ Repeat the quote, saying or mantra out loud several times
- ◆ Now Meditate. Set the timer for 6 min.
  - • Sit in a comfortable position. It can be on the floor, a chair or pillow. Most people cross their legs. Keep your back straight.
  - • Let your hands fall to your knees and rest them there gently, palms up. Alternatively, you can hold your hands together and rest them in the center of your lap.

- Breathe deeply thinking about the air flowing in and out of your nostrils. Fill up your lungs completely before exhaling. After a few intervals of deep breathing, breathe naturally, keeping your attention on the breath moving in and out and traveling throughout your body.
- When a thought enters your mind, distracting you from your breath, tell it to move on gently. If the thought feels urgent, tell it that you will go back to it at another time.
◆ When the timer goes off, open your eyes.
◆ Reread the quote.
◆ Individually reflect and write:
  - What does the quote mean to you?
  - How does it apply to your practice?
  - What questions do you have?
◆ Reflect on the following individually or with a partner:
  - What was your perception of the passing of time through-out the 6 min? Did it feel long or did time pass quickly? Could you have gone on longer?
  - What thoughts, feelings or images were occupying your mind?
  - In what way was this experience surprising or challenging?

2. Contemplating the Notion of Time

Purpose: To apply a contemplation strategy to a reading exercise in order to gain insight

Overview: Participants choose and contemplate a key phrase or sentence taken from a famous speech related to social justice

◆ You will need a copy of the speech and a timer.
  - Dr. Martin Luther King Jr., December 7, 1964, days before he received the Nobel Peace Prize in Oslo, King gave a major address in London on segregation https://www.democracy now.org/2017/1/16/newly_discovered_1964_mlk_speech_on
◆ Set the Intention: Non-Judgment.
  - An intention directs your attention and energy to an out-come. The outcome is typically a disposition, virtue or state of being.

- Sometimes, we connect an intention to a particular problem we want to solve, such as how to resolve a conflict with a student, boss or colleague. An intention of this nature would take the form of a statement such as "Using non-judgment in order to understand _____."
◆ Read the excerpt from one of Dr. Martin Luther King's speeches.[10]
    - If you have access to a speaker and the internet, you can also listen to the speech.
◆ Now, reread and annotate the text focusing on Time. Set the timer for 7–8 min.
    - Circle or underline any phrases or sentences that resonate with you and related in some way to the notion of time.
◆ When you are finished, choose one phrase or sentence to contemplate. For example,
    - Just be nice, be patient and continue to pray.
    - The appalling silence and indifference of the good people who sit around saying, "Wait on time."
◆ Contemplate in silence on this sentence or phrase. Set the timer for 3 min.
◆ Reflect and write the answers to the following questions or connect with a partner to discuss:
    - What came to mind when you were contemplating the phrase or sentence related to time?
    - What factors influence our perspective of time?
    - How does time influence our practice?
    - How can having a fixed perspective of time be harmful to others?

"I would like to mention one or two ideas that circulate in our society—and they probably circulate in your society and all over the world—that keep us from developing the kind of action programs necessary to get rid of discrimination and segregation. One is what I refer to as the myth of time. There are those individuals who argue that only time can solve the problem of racial injustice in the United States, in South Africa or anywhere else; you've got to wait for that time. And I know they've said to us so often in the United States and to our allies in the white community, "Just be nice and be patient and continue to pray, and in 100 or 200 years the problem will work itself out." We have heard and we have lived with the myth of time. The only answer that I can give to that myth is that time is neutral. It can be used either constructively or destructively. And I must honestly say to you that I'm convinced that the forces of ill will have often used time much more effectively than the forces of goodwill. And we may have to repent in this generation, not merely for the vitriolic words and the violent actions of the bad people, but for the appalling silence and indifference of the good people who sit around saying, "Wait on time."

And somewhere along the way it is necessary to see that human progress never rolls in on the wheels of inevitability. It comes through the tireless efforts and the persistent work of dedicated individuals who are willing to be co-workers with God. And without this hard work, time itself becomes an ally of the primitive forces of social stagnation. And so, we must help time, and we must realize that the time is always ripe to do right. This is so vital, and this is so necessary.

Connecting Strategy to Disposition

Reflective

- ◆ What feelings, thoughts and/or judgments seem to occupy your mind?
- ◆ What factors in your work environment influence your ability to be reflective?
- ◆ In what ways did these activities cultivate a reflective attitude?
- ◆ How can we encourage a reflective culture in our practice?

Strategy 2. Movement and Yoga

> Energy is the absolute source of inspiration and the impetus behind all personal and social transformation.[11]

My work requires sitting long hours at a desk to write and do research. Last year, my health faltered. I began to get chronic neck and back pain and numbness in my left arm. Since my work depends on my ability to write, I continued on as usual, ignoring my body. It was not until things worsened, and my work contract neared its end that I finally went to see a doctor. I got an MRI, a prescription and a recommendation for physical therapy. Shortly after, I lost my health benefits which motivated me to explore holistic and homeopathic methods. I began to practice yoga and exercise more regularly. I also meditated daily. In a short time, I became mindful of my posture, how I was walking and sitting. After two months, I had less pain and felt a surge of confidence. A few months later, with regular practice, my pain and the numbness in my arm disappeared, even though I was back to writing 4–5 hours a day.

Incorporating daily movement and yoga into your life has many health benefits, and it also teaches about the intricate relationship between the body, mind and spirit. When we engage in physical activity mindfully and practice yoga, we are stimulating the three domains for peak learning experience, which helps us to rise above or move beyond the physical plane. Knowing we can rise above the physical realm is a life saver when we are facing physical challenges or adverse conditions in our environment.

Movement includes physical activity such as walking, running, aerobics, bike riding, stretching, exercising, sports and so on. Physical activity outdoors or in green spaces has additional benefits. Moving your body outdoors feels less demanding, improves our mood, reduces stress and causes feelings of greater positive engagement.[12] Additionally, physical activity in a natural environment as compared to a climate-controlled space such as a school or gym increases our awareness of how climate impacts performance. If conditions are hot and humid or the landscape is mountainous, for example, runners quickly learn that they will tire out at a faster pace. For this reason, training for professional athletes involves learning how to adapt to and perform well in a wide range of conditions and environments. Our understanding of these nuances can lead to conscientious decision-making when it comes to planning, pacing or assessing performance.

Yoga is moving your body into various positions, holding still, breathing deeply and stretching. The positions of yoga are aligned to the seven vital energy centers of the body, called chakras. By balancing your chakras, energy flow is enhanced promoting health, a sense of well-being and vitality. The many benefits of yoga include the reduction of stress (decrease in cortisol), improved health and well-being, increased self-awareness, compassion, self-regulation, coping skills, strength, flexibility and balance. Observation, self-report surveys, participant feedback, program evaluations and self-studies reveal a consensus of firsthand experience bearing witness to the positive effects of yoga on themselves and others. These informants include teachers, principals and students. Furthermore, yoga is arguably one of the most inclusive and equitable practices because it can be learned by anyone, it can be passed on from person to person, it requires no equipment, it can be performed in very little space, there is no competition involved and there is no prerequisite form or ability to engage.[13]

Activities

1. Learning from the Great Outdoors

Purpose: To engage in an outdoor activity to learn about the relationship between the mind-body-spirit and how we are influenced by our environment

Overview: Participants go on a walk or run outdoors and reflect on the experience

- ◆ You will need a timer and comfortable shoes or sneakers.
- ◆ Plan for a brisk walk or a slow jog outdoors.
  - Choose an environment that has hills.
  - If possible, go to a park or a natural environment with greenery.
- ◆ Before any movement, set the intention to Focus. Set the timer for 4 min.
- ◆ Reflect and jot down short answers to the following:
  - How are you feeling? What is your emotional state?
  - How would you describe your attitude or mood?
  - What is on your mind?

- How does your body feel?
- How would you describe your level of energy?
◆ Start the brisk walk or jog. Set the timer for 30 min.
  - If you walk or run outdoors often, you can set the timer for longer.
◆ Immediately after, individually think and write:
  - How are you feeling now? What is your emotional state?
  - How would you describe your attitude or mood?
  - What is on your mind?
  - How does your body feel?
  - How would you describe your level of energy?
◆ Discuss with a partner:
  - What conditions in the environment can impact our level of energy?
  - How do our thoughts impact our energy?
  - How can movement change energy levels and our way of thinking?

2. Yoga

Purpose: To practice yoga to learn about the relationship between the mind-body-spirit and balance

Overview: Participants engage in a yoga exercise and reflect on the experience

◆ You will need enough space to spread out, comfortable clothing and the chakra and yoga positions chart.
  - Yoga mats, wood floors, grass (if outdoors).
  - You can choose to incorporate music for this activity, light, slow tempo and instrumental.
  - Athletic clothing, spandex. (Clothing should allow for a wide range of movement while also covering the body if in a public space.)
  - Barefoot or socks. (Socks can be slippery depending on the surface.)
◆ Find a quiet corner of the room with enough space to spread out.
◆ Set an intention: Balance.
  - For yoga, the intention should always start with Balance.

- As you gain confidence with the practice, the intention can move to other virtues or disposition such as inner peace, patience and awareness.
- Even in yoga, we can connect an intention to a particular problem you want to solve, such as thinking about how to be resolve a conflict with a student, boss or colleague.
- Advanced practice in yoga may involve adding the repetition of a mantra.
◆ Read the chart and choose one chakra and position to start on.
  - Review the Signs of Imbalance section and use this as an opportunity to target that area.
◆ Move yourself into the desired position, and hold, breathing slowly.
◆ Count slowly to 30, while holding the position.
  - You can adjust the length of hold time according to comfort with the position.
  - Don't strain or pull muscles unnecessarily.
  - Balance and stamina increase over time with practice.
◆ Repeat as often as you like, or move to another position. Set the timer for 8 min.
◆ When you are finished, reflect on the following in writing or with a partner:
  - What chakra and position did you decide to focus on? Why?
  - How did it feel holding yourself in a position for that length of time?
  - What was the nature of your thoughts and state of mind while you were holding the position?
  - How will you know when you are balanced and the natural flow of energy has improved?

Connecting Strategy to Disposition

Focused

◆ What types of feelings and thoughts seem to occupy your mind?
◆ In what ways did these activities support your ability to focus and minimize distractions?
◆ What about these activities did you find challenging or uncomfortable?
◆ What outside influences can limit our ability to focus?

Chakra Chart and Yoga Positions

Chakra	Overview	Yoga Positions
Crown Chakra **Union**	**Color**: Violet or White **Location**: Top of the head **Description**: Associated with enlightenment, spiritual growth, higher self, liberation, universal consciousness, selflessness, bliss, Oneness **Signs of Imbalance**: Associated with lack of meaning, apathy, depression, fatigue, hypersensitivity to environment, hyper-materialism	Lotus Tree
Third Eye Chakra	**Color:** Indigo **Location:** Forehead, Between and above the eyes **Description:** Associated with intuition, foresight, clear vision, openness, imagination, wisdom, direction, purpose, clairvoyance, dreams, telepathy **Signs of Imbalance:** Associated with anxiety, overanalytical, fearful, lack of concentration, feeling overwhelmed, aimlessness, confusion	Downward Dog Standing Forward Bend
Throat Chakra	**Color:** Turquoise **Location:** Throat, Neck **Description:** Associated with self-expression, communication, sharing ideas, telling the truth, processing information **Signs of Imbalance:** Associated with lack of expression, dishonesty, low self-esteem, extreme shyness, withdrawn, arrogant	Bridge Shoulder Stand

(Continued)

Chakra	Overview	Yoga Positions
Heart Chakra	**Color:** Green **Location:** Center of the chest **Description:** Associated with compassion, kindheartedness, love, relationships, self-acceptance, deep emotions **Signs of Imbalance:** Associated with insensitivity, sorrow, possessiveness, suspicion, resentment, dependency, difficulty in relationships, lack of self-discipline	Spinal Twist Cobra
Solar Plexus Chakra	**Color:** Yellow **Location:** Upper abdomen **Description:** Associated with identity and personal power, assertiveness, inner drive, sense of vitality, self-esteem, will-power, discipline, ego **Signs of Imbalance:** Associated with anger, uncertainty, fear of rejection, indecisiveness, low self-esteem, resentment, perfectionism, hypersensitive to criticism, concern with status	Bow Archer
Sacral Chakra	**Color:** Orange **Location:** Lower abdomen, Lower back, Sexual organs **Description:** Associated with self-worth, sexuality, creativity, fluidity, openness, pleasure, intimacy, confidence, warmth **Signs of Imbalance:** Associated with being out of touch with feelings, poor boundaries, overly emotional, frustration, overly stoic, repressed creativity, sexual dysfunction, isolation	Bound Angle Wide Squat

Chakra	Overview	Yoga Positions
Root Chakra	**Color:** Red	Child's Pose
	Location: Base of spine, Perineum	
	Description: Associated with our basic animal instinct for survival, self-preservation, shelter, food, health, money, sense of belonging, safety, security, stability, the physical world	Lunge Pose
	Signs of Imbalance: Associated with fear, vulnerability, insecurity, distrust, greed, grief, worry, anxiety, self-centeredness, scattered energy	

Source: Adapted from The Chakra Deck, Written by Olivia H. Miller, Chronicle Books, San Francisco, 2004.

Strategy 3. Identity and Culture Study

The full integration of the personal and the professional self must exist if we want to transform our practice.[14]

When I bring up the topic of identity and culture in the professional space, I find that educators have become saturated by identity boxes and fixed labels, especially young people. Now, more than ever, students are identifying as mixed-race or do not identify with any race category at all. The latter is especially true for Hispanics, according to recent Census Bureau research. Racial categories, which have been included on every US census since the first one in 1790, have changed from decade to decade. Educators continue to struggle when approaching the topic of identity and culture, as well as how to adjust their language respectfully. The struggle is partly due to our history of oppression, racism, xenophobia and homophobia, but it is also because identity and culture are not static, linear or fixed. They combine subjective and intersubjective systems, meaning the way people form their sense of self does not happen apart from other people immersed in structures of power.[15]

Identity and culture are dynamic, multifaceted, embedded in context, influenced by social, economic and political factors, socially constructed, learned and dialectical. Culture is not a given but a human creation, dependent on particular geographical, temporal and sociopolitical contexts, and therefore vulnerable to issues of power and control.[16] Understanding the fluidity of identity and culture and the relationship to learning and how we engage in society is critical, especially when identity politics and the media try to reduce human experience to one fixed, racialized or gendered category. Teaching that a person can occupy multiple dimensions of identity and experience both privilege and disadvantage at the same time, for example, can soften resistance to being reflective and reveal the complexity of human identity and the notion of intersectionality.[17]

The brain is constantly shaped and reshaped by our interactions with the surrounding environment.[18] Interactions that engender fear, trauma, stress, hate, shame, low self-esteem impact cognition and our ability to respond to situations wisely. These experiences are endemic and indicative of an inequitable society. When we approach our work from a holistic perspective, we want to raise awareness of societal factors, while simultaneously empowering students to direct their attention and energy away from the lower, Root Chakra (associated with vulnerability, fear, anxiety, preoccupation with survival and self-preservation). Our work, therefore, involves designing learning experiences that move students into the higher chakra regions where love, personal power, compassion and purpose live. Designing learning from this standpoint assumes we have the power and the control to direct the flow of energy and information, and we can choose, at any time, a higher moral orientation, independent of external factors.

By looking at Figure 3.2, you will see the Pathway to Transcendence, which is the pathway to rise above the lower, survival modes of experience through sustained attention and investigation into altered states of being and consciousness to higher modes of experience towards liberation and selflessness.

The strategy Identity and Culture Study is not just about cultivating consciousness or personal awareness, but rather

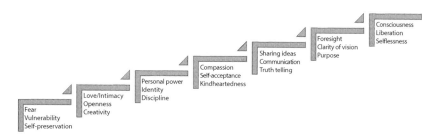

FIGURE 3.2 The Path to Transcendence.

developing a critical consciousness and learning how to redirect attention and energy to where we have the most leverage. This involves an awareness of the intersectionality of factors that contribute to and influence a person's feelings about culture and identity, and how all these elements influence our ability to trust, our readiness to learn and our capacity to process information. It is about designing learning experiences that focus on developing self-assuredness and applying personal power to purpose.

Activities

1. Know Thyself

Purpose: To engage in a creative, image-based activity to explore identity and culture and to learn how these activities can trigger an emotional response

Overview: Participants draw a portrait of themselves in a setting from their childhood and reflect on the meaning and contents of the drawing

- ◆ You will need a pencil, a large piece of paper, a set of markers or another colorful art medium. You will also need a timer.
- ◆ Draw a picture of yourself in the setting of your childhood.
  - • Make sure it is a full-length portrait.
  - • The background should be the residence/neighborhood where you grew up.
  - • Illustrate your physical traits, attributes, characteristics.

- Use symbols to represent elements of your identity that may not be so apparent, such as religion/spiritual beliefs, social status/class, language, talents/powers and sexual orientation.
◆ When you are finished, contemplate your drawing. Set the timer for 3 min.
◆ Set an intention: Personal Awareness.
  - An intention directs your attention and energy to an outcome. The outcome is typically a disposition, virtue or state of being.
  - Sometimes, we connect an intention to a particular problem we want to solve, such as how to resolve a conflict with a student, boss or colleague. An intention of this nature would take the form of a statement such as "Using personal awareness in order to understand_____."
◆ Put the drawing down and contemplate your identity. Set the timer for 5 min.
◆ Now, return to your drawing and circle the identity elements in your picture that you think have given you advantages, power or privilege in society.
◆ Put a box around the identity elements you think have made things more difficult for you, have limited you in some way or have put you at a disadvantage in society.
◆ Individually or with a partner, reflect on the following questions while looking at your drawing:
  - How do you describe yourself?
  - What symbols did you use to illustrate your personality and other not so apparent attributes of your identity?
  - How do you describe your childhood residence/ neighborhood? How did this environment influence how you see yourself and the world?
  - When did you first realize that some elements of your identity gave you advantages or privileges in life?
  - When did you realize that some aspects of your identity can limit you in some ways?
  - What emotions did you notice when you engaged in this activity?

2. A Musical Glimpse into Culture

Purpose: To learn how music is both universal and a cultural form of expression

Overview: Participants listen to a favorite song and analyze it

- ◆ Choose one of your favorite songs, preferably from your teenage years. Have the music handy.
- ◆ You will also need a copy of the graphic Path to Transcendence and a timer.
- ◆ Get into a comfortable position.
- ◆ Set an intention: Deep Listening.
  - • An intention directs your attention and energy to an outcome. The outcome is typically a disposition, virtue or state of being.
  - • Sometimes, we connect an intention to a particular problem we want to solve, such as how to resolve a conflict with a student, boss or colleague. An intention of this nature would take the form of a statement such as "Using deep listening in order to understand_____."
- ◆ Plan to listen to the song for more than just lyrics. You will listen to the melody, rhythm and tempo.
- ◆ Play the song and close your eyes while listening.
- ◆ When you are finished, look at the key terms on the Path to Transcendence graphic and think about the song's main message.
  - • For example, is the song about love and intimacy or liberation?
  - • If you can't match the message to any of the terms outlined on the Path to Transcendence, in your own words, describe the main message of the song.
- ◆ Close your eyes and quietly contemplate the main message of the song. Set the timer for 3 min.
- ◆ Now, listen to the song for a second time. Think about the unique identity and culture of the artist.
  - • Consider all aspects of culture and identity, including language, country of origin, gender, sexual orientation, age/

        generational affiliation, race/ethnicity, language, physical traits of artist, religion or spiritual outlook and so on.

◆ When the song is finished, reflect individually in writing or discuss with a partner:

    ● What elements of culture and identity influence how the artist expresses the main message?

    ● Do you think this song has "universal" appeal? Why or why not?

◆ To extend learning, you can search out songs from other cultures that communicate the same message. This is a fun way to appreciate other cultures and increase your awareness of universal themes.

Connecting Strategy to Disposition

Self-Assured

◆ In what ways did these activities help you appreciate your character, identity and culture?

◆ What aspects of yourself do you need to appreciate more to build confidence?

◆ How can we create inclusive learning environments where people appreciate each other's unique culture and abilities?

Strategy 4. Acting and Performance

> When I walk into a room full of educators there is always a moment of pause when I ask myself, why am I here? What is the most important thing?[19]

My work frequently involves observing and giving feedback to educators who facilitate professional learning. Role-play is a common strategy I see. It's a fun way to get students to interact with each other, explore a topic and apply new learning. On one occasion, an observation of a role-play revealed just how much acting and performance can give us insight into who we are, how we see the world and what we think is important. In a session on behavior management, the facilitator asked the faculty to demonstrate a typical interaction between a teacher and a student. Partners got up, one by one, and performed. To my surprise, several of the teachers portrayed elements of the students' culture in crude and disparaging ways. The room filled with laughter. Everyone was trying to figure out who was the student. Names of boys and girls pop-corned into the air. At the end, the facilitator applauded their enthusiasm and much to my chagrin, never mentioned the words culture or bias in the debrief. I was reminded of Stanislavski, the famous Russian actor, director and teacher who wrote,

> You can never get away from yourself. The moment you lose yourself on stage marks the departure from truly living your part and the beginning of exaggerated false acting. Always and forever, when you are on stage, you must play yourself.[20]

Stanislavski is known for his acting method that focuses on authenticity and stage presence. He described it as being able to fit your own human qualities into the life of the character, to fully live the part. According to Stanislavsky, all authentic action must have a strong inner foundation; otherwise, it will never hold an audience's attention. Central to Stanislavski's method is becoming aware, clarifying purpose and stepping into the shoes of another human being. For these reasons, acting and performance techniques can be applied to our work cultivating Authentic Presence. Preparing for a theatrical performance can also lead us to consider the ethical dimensions related to our role by considering how action and behavior are consistent with core beliefs and purpose.[21]

Educators perform in front of others every day. That is why performance is a key component in how we are evaluated. What does it mean to perform in the context of education and to perform authentically? How can studying acting and performance techniques help us to inspire others and communicate purpose? Good performance is determined not only by our actions but by the impact they have on others, just like in the theater. The actors that have stage presence are the ones who hold our attention, make us feel something and open our mind to a different perspective. By applying Acting and Performance techniques to our professional learning, we begin to align our inner work with our outer performance, keeping in mind the impact we want to have on our audience.

Activities

1. Extemporaneous Speaking

Purpose: To build confidence speaking about an important topic to inspire others

Overview: Participants videotape themselves speaking on a topic with little preparation and analyze the results

- ◆ You will need a timer, a video camera and index cards.
- ◆ The objective of this activity is to prepare for and perform an impromptu speech about a topic in your field.
- ◆ Decide on a topic and frame it as a question.
  - • The more controversial or personally meaningful the topic the better.
  - • Examples: Should every school have a metal detector? Do you think teachers should earn more money? Is culturally relevant pedagogy appropriate for all schools?
- ◆ Set an intention: Communicating Your Truth.
  - • An intention directs your attention and energy to an outcome. The outcome is typically a disposition, virtue or state of being.
  - • Sometimes, we connect an intention to a particular problem we want to solve, such as how to resolve a conflict with a student, boss or colleague. An intention of this nature would take the form of a statement such as "Using my ability to communicate truth in order to resolve_____."
- ◆ Get into a comfortable position and contemplate the topic and your intention. Set the timer for 4 min.
- ◆ Write down a few thoughts/main points you want to include in your talk on an index card. Set the timer for 3 min.

- Introduce your topic and state the claim.
- Share two to three ideas to support your claim.
- Come to a conclusion.
◆ Set up the camera. Stand 2–3 feet away and speak. Set the timer for 5–7 min. Try to speak for the whole time.
◆ Review your presentation and reflect on the following questions:
  - What did you notice about yourself during the performance?
  - How was your tone, pacing and attitude?
  - How did you express emotion?
  - Did you appear relaxed? Why or why not?
  - How did you use body language or facial expressions?
  - How might you improve the next time?

2. Stepping into Character

Purpose: To learn a strategy to better understand the experience and perspective of another human being

Overview: Participants engage in a character study and perform the role in front of a camera

◆ You will need a timer; a video camera; a table; a chair; and a table setting for one, including cutlery, plate and glass.
◆ Think about someone in your professional community that you work with, support or directly report to. It can be a colleague, leader, student, parent and so on.
◆ Close your eyes and visualize this person in your mind. Set the timer for 5 min.
  - Physical characteristics;
  - Personality;
  - Attributes;
  - Behavior.
◆ Now think about the person at home. Set the timer for 3 min.
◆ Write down the answers to the following questions. If you know the answers, write them. Otherwise, fill in the blanks using your imagination. Set the timer for 7 min.
  - Do they live alone or with a family member, friend or roommate?

- Are they cooking dinner or going out to eat?
- Where do they live? Are they happy with their home or neighborhood? Do they feel safe, loved and comfortable?
- Are they reading, watching television, listening to music, exercising?
- Are they still in their work clothes, or did they change into pajamas or loungewear?
- What is their emotional state? Are they tired, stressed, nervous or relaxed? Are they satisfied with their work day or are they disappointed or discouraged?

◆ Consider the person's dreams and ambitions. Set the timer for 3 min.

◆ Write down the answers to the following questions. If you know the answers, write them; otherwise, fill in the blanks using your imagination.
- Does this person have aspirations?
- Are they currently working toward a goal?
- What did they want to be when they were young?
- What successes have they had in their life?
- What disappointments?

◆ Now, set the table with your props and set up the camera aiming at the table.

◆ Role-play this person eating a meal at home or at a casual restaurant on a typical work day. Set the timer for 10 min. You must perform until the timer goes off.

◆ Watch your performance on the videotape, and reflect on the following questions:
- What actions drove your performance?
- How did your preparation influence your behavior?
- How did you feel acting like this person?
- Do you think you were credible? Why or why not?

Connecting Strategy to Disposition

Inspiring

◆ What did you learn about your ability to communicate and inspire others?

◆ What factors in the environment may inhibit your ability to perform well?

- How can you build confidence in yourself as an inspirational public speaker?
- How can we support others to build confidence performing in front of others?

Assessing for Barriers

Authentic Presence makes us vulnerable. It is natural for us to tense up and pull back in an environment with low levels of trust. Learning organizations are evolving organisms, just like us. They are filled with contradictions and tensions related to culture and identity, the economy, politics, the demands of high-stakes testing and evaluations. It is no wonder we are afraid of letting go and being ourselves in these spaces.

When we are not authentic we normalize superficiality, hypocrisy, fear and anxiety. When we are not authentic, we are not building trusting relationships which, reduces our ability to build relationships and to teach with credibility. If we can't model Authentic Presence for our students, how will they know it is possible to bring their whole self into the education space and to be seen, loved and to feel useful? We are the beacons of light and possibility.

Stress

Stress is evoked by fear of a perceived threat to safety, status or well-being. Cortisol is often called the stress hormone. A normal amount of cortisol is actually good for you. It plays an important role in your metabolism and gives you the energy you need to respond to a threatening situation or challenge. However, too much cortisol diminishes our cognitive ability and chronic stress makes us prone to illness.

In addition to meditation, yoga and movement, here are some ways you can reduce stress:

- Detach physically from stress trigger.
- Go to the ocean or a mountain.
- Get hugs and physical affection.
- Play games and act silly.
- Plant and touch the soil.
- Dance and play music.

+ Laugh and have fun.
+ Listen to stories.
+ Make art.
+ Howl.

Fear

Threats, whether perceived or real, result in neurobiological changes that impact our behavior, performance and cognitive abilities. There are numerous types of threats that affect our ability to be authentic and present that are not so apparent, such as stereotype threats and status threats. Research in neuroscience has shown that we are affected by the way we feel we are seen and judged by others. When we expect to be viewed as inferior, are abilities seem to be diminished. Chemicals in the brain, such as dopamine, adrenaline, serotonin and cortisol, impact our memory, our attention, our ability to problem solve, our mood and our ability to perform at our best.[22]

Paying attention to our emotional responses, identifying triggers and applying self-care strategies can help combat your fears. Here is a list of self-care strategies:

+ Become a master in your field.
+ Attribute success to your own abilities.
+ Spend time with people who believe in your potential.
+ Beautify your surroundings.
+ Find and study role models.
+ Put your personal safety and health first.
+ Keep someone close who challenges you.
+ Invest in relationships with people from diverse backgrounds.
+ Travel and explore other neighborhoods.
+ Dress for success.

Activity

Take a moment to think about the learning and activities from this chapter, and fill out this chart by considering potential barriers and next steps. At the start of this chapter, I shared three barriers: fear, hypocrisy and impatience. This is not an exhaustive list. Trust yourself and your feelings as you process your learning. Use the example for guidance.

Strategy	Potential Barrier/s	Next Steps
Contemplation and Meditation	Example: Impatience	Example: Reduce the amount of time for each activity and increase gradually
Movement and Yoga		
Identity and Culture Study		
Acting and Performance		

Application to Practice: Planning Tool

The following is a *tool* to help you plan and coach others in their planning. It is important to remember that all three domains involve contemplative practices, discoveries, dispositions and awareness that are nonlinear and subtle. For this reason, the use of tools or instruments for planning, observation or assessment should be considered entry points for discussion and analysis.

Planning for Learning Experience Tool

Name	Date
Learning Outcomes	

Content	Notes
• What knowledge about Authentic Presence is essential? • What skills and dispositions do I want students to have? • What vocabulary and terminologies should students know? • What books, texts and resources will support learning? • What assignments and performance tasks will lead to Authentic Presence? • How will I assess for conceptual understanding and application of the four strategies?	
Pedagogy • How will I make connections between Authentic Presence and other topics in this course? • How can students practice Authentic Presence in the real world? • How will I model this practice? • How will I differentiate instruction and personalize learning? • How much time will I build in for reflection and contemplation? • How will I monitor and recognize progress? • What challenges, misconceptions or barriers do I anticipate? • How will I prepare for these barriers?	
Environment • What norms and protocols support this domain? • How will I create a flexible learning space that is inspiring? • What opportunities are there to go outside? • How will I support Authentic Presence when using technology or virtual platforms?	

Checking In

Go back to your Initial Self-Assessment. Review your answers to Part I. Authentic Presence. Reflect on the following questions:

- ♦ What are three things you learned about Authentic Presence?
- ♦ Why are Personal Awareness and Self-Mastery important?
- ♦ What aspect of this domain do you want to concentrate on moving forward?
- ♦ How can we encourage Authentic Presence in the workplace?
- ♦ What questions do you still have?

Notes

1 Rios, R. (2017) *Teacher Agency for Equity: A Framework for Conscientious Engagement*. Routledge, New York, p. 117.

2 Rios, R. (2017) *Teacher Agency for Equity: A Framework for Conscientious Engagement*. Routledge, New York, p. 86.

3 Siegel, D. (2007) *The Mindful Brain, Mind Your Brain*. W. W. Norton & Company Inc., New York & London, p. 13.

4 Siegel, D. (2007) *The Mindful Brain, Mind Your Brain*. W. W. Norton & Company Inc., New York & London, p. 262.

5 Ergas, O. (2018) A contemplative turn in education: Charting a curricular pedagogical countermovement, *Pedagogy, Culture & Society (ahead of print)*.

6 Lama, D. (2006) *The Universe in a Single Atom: The Convergence of Science and Spirituality*. Digital. Harmony reprint edition. Location 131 of 2448.

7 Bashar, P. (2016) Different Cultures See Deadlines Differently, *Harvard Business Review*. Retrieved from https://hbr.org/2016/05/different-cultures-see-deadlines-differently

8 Fontana, D. (1999) *Learn to Meditate: A Practical Guide to Self-Discovery and Fulfillment*. Chronicle Books, San Francisco, CA, p. 16.

9 Retrieved from www.goodreads.com/author/quotes/6134. Arundhati_Roy

10 Dr. Martin Luther King Jr., December 7, 1964, days before he received the Nobel Peace Prize in Oslo, King gave a major address

in London on segregation. Retrieved from www.democracynow.
org/2017/1/16/newly_discovered_1964_mlk_speech_on

11 Rios, R. (2017) *Teacher Agency for Equity: A Framework for Conscientious Engagement*. Routledge, New York, p. 101.

12 Gladwell, V.F., Brown, D.K., Wood, C., Sandercock, G.R. and Barton, J.L. (2013) The Great Outdoors: How a Green Exercise Environment Can Benefit All, *Extreme Physiology & Medicine*, Vol. 2, p. 3. doi:10.1186/2046-7648-2-3

13 Hyde, A. (2012) The Yoga in Schools Movement: Using Standards for Educating the Whole Child and Making Space for Teacher Self-Care, *Counterpoints*, Vol. 425, pp. 109–126. Retrieved from www.jstor.org/stable/42981793

14 Rios, R. (2017) *Teacher Agency for Equity: A Framework for Conscientious Engagement*. Routledge, New York, p. 16.

15 Sánchez-Flores, M.J. (2017) Mindfulness and Complex Identities in Equity Training: A Pilot Study, *European Review of Applied Sociology*, Vol. 10, No. 14, p. 23.

16 Nieto, S. (2008) *Culture and Education. In Yearbook for the National Society for the Study of Education*. Blackwell Publishing, Hoboken, NJ.

17 Sánchez-Flores, M.J. (2017) Mindfulness and Complex Identities in Equity Training: A Pilot Study, *European Review of Applied Sociology*, Vol. 10, No. 14, p. 20.

18 Rose, D. et al. (2011/2012) The Universal Design for Learning Framework to Support Culturally Diverse Learners, *Journal of Education*, Vol. 192, No. 1, pp. 17–22.

19 Rios, R. (2017) *Teacher Agency for Equity: A Framework for Conscientious Engagement*. Routledge, New York, pp. 109–110.

20 Stanislavski, C. (1937) *Constantin Stanislavski: An Actor Prepares*. Translated by E.R. Hapgood, A Methuen Paperback, London, p. 177.

21 Aponte-Moreno, M. (2014) *Embodying Authentic Leadership: An Actor's Perspective, Leading with Spirit, Presence and Authenticity*. Edited by K.G. Schuyler, Jossey-Bass Inc., San Francisco, CA, p. 201.

22 Wilkinson, R. and Pickett, K. (2010) *The Spirit Level, Why Greater Equality Makes Societies Stronger*. Bloomsbury Press, New York & London, p. 113.

Freedom

Social Awareness and Adaptability

Courage, creativity and innovation can flourish in organic relationships that come together through spirit consciousness.[1]

We are entangled with some people more than others, and these relationships impact how we behave in the world. Freedom is about choosing to engage or disengage with people (or situations) in order to move into alignment with the authentic self. Social Awareness and Adaptability lead to the practice of Freedom. They entail learning about relationships, group dynamics and power as well as how norms, systems and institutions function in society. We experience freedom when we are seen, acknowledged and appreciated for who we really are; when we feel trust and belonging in social situations; and when we feel we are worthy and useful in society. When we can move into different spaces, adapt ourselves without losing our sense of self and purpose and collaborate with others across cultural differences towards a common goal, we discover the joy of freedom. In this chapter, we explore four strategies that lead to the practice of Freedom. We engage in activities, reflect on our experience and consider how we can apply freedom to our practice.

The following are dispositions and barriers associated with freedom to recognize and anticipate. At the end of each strategy, you will be prompted to think about a disposition to process your learning. At the end of the chapter, you will have the opportunity to synthesize your experience, consider barriers and apply to practice.

Dispositions

Trustworthy: When people can rely and depend on you to be honest, dedicated and committed;

Inclusive: Creating a space where everyone feels included and feels a sense of belonging;

Responsive: Adapting our approach or behavior to meet the needs of an individual, group or situation;

Compassionate: The willingness to listen deeply and bear witness to the suffering of others, and to help relieve that suffering.

Barriers

Guilt: When a person believes or realizes they have done something wrong because the behavior goes against their own values or a universal moral standard;

Isolation: Feeling alone, disconnected and separate from others;

Rigidity: Being fixed and unwavering in our thinking and approach to people and situations;

Shame: A feeling of disgrace and humiliation that occurs when we attribute a moral transgression to ourselves.

Strategy 1. Intergroup Dialogue

Last year, I attended an anti-racist training out in California. I didn't want to attend and neither did many of my colleagues. We were emotionally, physically and spiritually fatigued by the topic of race in education. Then a colleague told me, "When you receive an invitation to such an event, it is not just an invitation for you. It is an invitation for you, your forefathers, your ancestors, who without your presence remain voiceless and unrepresented."[2] I appreciated his comment and went with a different perspective.

Intergroup dialogue is a necessary vehicle for understanding identity, culture, knowledge and normative shared values and beliefs among members of groups. The effectiveness of an organization will ultimately depend on its ability to communicate across cultures and subcultures. Intergroup dialogue can improve communication across differences and lead to a common language and the discovery of new mental models needed for personal and social transformation.

With so many benefits, why does intergroup dialogue often cause us stress and anxiety? Human beings will go to great lengths to maintain social bonds, to avoid pain and suffering, to protect their public image and ward off any threat to their survival, real or perceived. Trust is a requirement for intergroup dialogue, and trust takes time to cultivate—especially when there are unresolved issues related to our history of racism and oppression. People will naturally experience a wide range of uncomfortable emotions when they first engage in intergroup dialogue. Some may experience guilt due to their privileged social location ascribed to them by societal structures that they themselves did nothing to produce, but from which they benefit nonetheless.[3] Others may experience anger or shame. We become hypersensitive when our social structure and economy is based on competition, and we feel the need to fight for what is ours to survive.

Policy and practice in education are so intertwined with human rights, freedom and equality that it is impossible for educators not to feel the weight and complexity of these conversations. Now, young people are coming to the table with a different perspective and nomenclature. Each generation advances; sometimes we take steps back. There are forces moving us one way or another that often feel beyond our control. For this reason, it is essential we develop patience, tolerance and compassion for dialogue with people who look, feel and think differently than ourselves. If we cannot reduce the level of stress and anxiety associated with these courageous conversations, we will avoid them, and when we don't engage, we will never be in the position to teach the practice of Freedom to others with authenticity.

We can ease our way through the discomfort by recognizing and anticipating barriers to Authentic Presence, such as bias, judgments, fear, impatience and hypocrisy. In this way, we depersonalize experience and understand that there are feelings and experiences that we all share to some degree or another. When we take ourselves out from the center of the experience and make it a human experience, we begin to really listen and share openly.

Deep listening and bearing witness to the suffering of others in dialogue, which involves suspending judgment, transforms each person in the room into a vessel for healing and reciprocal transformation. Paradoxically, when we do this, we are at the center of change. Through dialogue, we are challenging norms, structures and systems that perpetuate inequities, and we are exploring new structures by which we can envision and create a future that does not exist and discover our part in bringing that future to pass.[4,5]

Activities

1. Storytelling

Purpose: To practice being honest in front of a group and deep listening

Overview: Each person will share a personal story while the group listens

- ◆ You will need a quiet room with no interruptions, a timer and a group of three to five people.
  - Sit comfortably in a circle so everyone can see each other.
- ◆ Have someone volunteer to be the timekeeper and facilitator.
  - The facilitator is responsible for keeping time, opening and closing the dialogue and reading any instructions or materials.
- ◆ Open the dialogue by thanking everybody for their presence. Share the purpose of the dialogue and give instructions.
  - Each person will get 3–4 min to share a personal story about a time they felt isolated or as if they didn't belong to a group because of their identity, culture or way of being.
  - The group will practice Deep Listening strategies:
    1. Listen for thoughts and use of language.
    2. Listen for feelings and relationships.
    3. Listen for insights and emerging ideas.

- When the person is done sharing, the group can ask clarifying questions.
◆ Before sharing, take a few minutes to contemplate the intention: Deep Listening. Set the timer for 3 min.
  - An intention directs your attention and energy to an outcome. The outcome is typically a disposition, virtue or state of being.
  - Sometimes, we connect an intention to a particular problem we want to solve, such as how to resolve a conflict with a student, boss or colleague. An intention of this nature would take the form of a statement such as "By listening deeply, I want to_____."

◆ Go around the circle. Each person shares. Set the timer for 20 min.
◆ After the last person shares, the facilitator should instruct the group to close their eyes for a closing meditation. Set the timer for 5 min.
◆ After the timer goes off, the facilitator should instruct the group to reflect individually in writing on the following questions:

  - How did it feel to share your personal story in front of a group?
  - What was your experience listening deeply?
  - What did you learn about the nature of belonging?
  - What did the stories reveal about identity and culture?
  - What is one thing we can do in our practice to create a more inclusive environment?

2. Learning from History

Purpose: To engage in an intergroup dialogue to practice new norms and build trust

Overview: Participants examine two sources about history, engage in an intergroup dialogue and make connections to practice

◆ You will need access to a computer with internet connection, a speaker, chart paper or a whiteboard, a timer and a group of at least three people.

- Choose one person who will act as the facilitator.
  - Communicates details with participants prior to dialogue.
  - Sends links and materials.
  - Reviews norms, process and manages the flow of activities.
- The group should arrive having accessed the multimedia sources for reading and listening.
  - Read: https://www.history.com/topics/black-history/ brown-v-board-of-education-of-topeka
  - Listen to: http://revisionisthistory.com/ episodes/13-miss-buchanans-period-of-adjustment
- The facilitator writes the guiding questions on the chart paper or board.
  - In what ways do schools and education systems perpetuate inequities in society?
  - What can we learn from history to help us disrupt inequities today?
- Introduce Norms (See Norms for Conscientious Engagement.)
  1. Be authentic and present.
  2. Listen deeply.
  3. Be deliberate.
  4. Stay open and receptive.
  5. Create sacred space.
- The facilitator asks the group if they would like to add any norms.
- Set the intention: Compassion.
- Instruct the group to contemplate in silence on the intention. Set the timer for 3 min.
  - An intention directs attention and energy to an outcome. The outcome is typically a disposition, virtue or state of being.
  - The facilitator should remind the group that Compassion is the willingness to listen deeply and bear witness to the suffering of others and to help relieve suffering.
- Play the media source for the group.
  - Listen: http://revisionisthistory.com/episodes/13-miss -buchanans-period-of-adjustment
  - Use the Deep Listening strategies:

1. Listen for thoughts and use of language.
2. Listen for feelings and relationships.
3. Listen for insight and emerging ideas.

◆ Read the guiding question aloud and ask for a volunteer to start. Set the timer for 25 min.
  • In what ways do school systems perpetuate inequities in society?
◆ Facilitator supports the dialogue by
  • Ensuring equity of voice.
  • Encouraging participants to refer to the sources.
  • Asking clarifying questions.
  • Jotting down main ideas on the board or chart paper.
◆ The facilitator introduces the second question when there is a natural lull in the conversation.
  • How can we disrupt these inequities in the context of education today?
◆ When the timer goes off, the facilitator wraps up the discussion.
◆ Engage in a closing meditation. Set the timer for 5 min.
◆ Each person individually reflects and writes an answer to the guiding questions. Set the timer for 10 min.
  • What can we learn about the role schools and educational institutions play in perpetuating inequities in society by studying history?
  • How can we disrupt these inequities in the context of education today?
◆ Debrief with the whole group.
  • What insights did you have?
  • In what ways did the dialogue help you to understand the topic?

Connecting Strategy to Disposition

Trustworthy

◆ How does deep listening lead to trust?
◆ Why is it difficult to trust each other at work?
◆ How do you know a person is trustworthy?

Norms for Conscientious Engagement

1. **Be authentic and present**: Be yourself, trust your intuition, stay focused.
2. **Listen deeply:** Listen for thoughts, feelings, relationships and insight.
3. **Be deliberate:** Be intentional and consider the impact of your words.
4. **Stay open and receptive:** Notice emerging ideas.
5. **Create sacred space:** Be respectful, compassionate and empowering.

Strategy 2. Rituals and Ceremony

> Agency for equity is often operationalized through an individual's willingness to confront the forces of group dynamics.[6]

The boardroom was set up with sticky note pads, chart paper, little notebooks, water bottles and coffee. We were anxious to get to work. It was time to check in on our progress and strategize. Next to the fourth bullet on the agenda, I noticed a team building activity. I began to panic. Things had not been going smoothly in our team for several weeks. There was miscommunication about roles, responsibilities and expectations as well as clashes in style and personality. When the meeting started, I forgot about team building. Shortly after lunch, when we were full and drowsy, the director jumped up and announced that it was time. She popped a song into our audio system and instructed us to get up and dance. The team building activity had begun and all I wanted to do was crawl under the table and vanish.

The human spirit yearns for belonging, active participation, a rhyme and reason for being and an understanding of the magical forces that bring us together in relationship. Instinctively, we are drawn together like insects to light. We set a time and place to meet; we share, corroborate, express reverence for living. We learn that when we combine our energy we have the power to set a special moment apart, to honor an individual or accomplishment that would otherwise go unnoticed in the rapid passing of time.

Building authentic relationships across cultural differences, making meaningful connections with others and feeling a part of a community have become strained. This is due to a cocktail of ingredients including technology and the internet, a modern economy that does not involve us working at the same job or location for long periods of time, demographic shifts and increasing diversity and a rise in xenophobia. All of these factors have raised important questions about how to build community and find common ground in organizations and modern society.

Learning organizations and institutions have always relied on built-in rituals, customs and ceremonies that bring people together. However, all across the country there are signs that we are reexamining our values. Educators and practitioners in the helping professions realize we need new mental models, new modes of communication and community outreach. It is time to consider what kinds of rituals and ceremonies will communicate a new way of being, a new vision for society.

A ritual is a set of behaviors designed to produce the desired effect, such as joy and celebration, gratitude, recognition, appreciation, healing, honor, pride or tribute. A ritual can be individual and personal such as lighting candles and sitting on a pillow for prayer or meditation or and it can be communal such as a morning meeting. A ceremony is a ritual with greater formality and public recognition. Behind every ritual and ceremony is the wisdom that if we pause our daily routine and behave deliberately, we validate and exalt human experience. Rituals and ceremonies have the potential to enrich our lives by creating sacred space and paying tribute to what we value. It is an intentional setting aside a time and place to enact our beliefs. For organizations, these moments provide us with the opportunity to publicly recognize excellence and achievement which leads to trust[7] and worthiness.

Social, cultural and political dynamics influence our feelings about and attachment to rituals. Some rituals that are inherited are problematic when looked at through the lens of equity and social justice. If a ritual contradicts with one's own values and beliefs; appears superficial, hypocritical or contrived; or reflects oppressive ideologies, participating in it can cause distress and suffering for an individual or communities. Refusing to engage, in these cases, is an act of courage, freedom and self-determination. We saw this at play on the national stage when Colin Kaepernick refused to kneel during the national anthem to draw attention to police brutality and the assault on black lives. His refusal to engage in this national ritual was so symbolic that it became a full-scale act of civil disobedience. There are smaller, less public acts of freedom that people do every day. Women, for example, who refuse certain rituals in the home are challenging outdated gender roles.

As we evolve individually and as a nation, it is important to resist the temptation to do away with rituals and ceremonies in order to avoid conflict. How will we build trust and community otherwise? Instead, we need to increase our awareness of the undercurrents of change and commit to new ways of being and doing, both in private and in public settings. We do have the potential and the capacity to build trust in one another, to live authentically without fear, to love and respect one another, to honor and pay tribute to excellence and accomplishment, and all of this, we can accomplish through the process of education.

Activities

1. The Circle of Trust

Purpose: To learn how certain actions, language and group behaviors build trust and community

Overview: Participants engage in a ritual and reflect on the emotional response

1. You will need a group of no more than ten participants, a room large enough for everyone to stand comfortably in a circle, a facilitator and a wand.
    *   A wand is a tool that invokes the use of superpowers and affirms our belief in our potential to create and manifest our ideas into reality.
    *   Wands can be any material and any size.
    *   A wand can be bought or created.
    *   The ideal wand carries your energy which comes from the time and care you put into the process.
2. The facilitator should put the wand in the center of the room with the tip of the wand facing North.
3. The facilitator starts by explaining that they will engage in a ritual to build trust and community.
4. Ask the group to stand around the wand in a circle formation for a standing meditation.
    *   Each person should stand facing the group with their arms by their side in a comfortable, relaxed stance.
    *   The group should feel free throughout the meditation to look at each other.
5. Set the intention: *Trust*. Set the timer for 3 min.
    *   An intention directs your attention and energy to an outcome. The outcome is typically a disposition, virtue or state of being.
    *   For this activity, it is advisable to start with a simple intention of Trust, and being present.
6. After the timer goes off, the facilitator explains that they will now honor the four directions of earth that represent important life energies[8] by turning in unison in that direction.
    *   Say: North represents the element Air and the life energy Power.
        1. Have everyone face in the direction the wand is pointing to, North.
        2. Pause and hold for a silent count of ten.
    *   Say: South represents the element Earth and the life energy Love.
        1. Have everyone face in the opposite direction, South.
        2. Pause and hold for a silent count of ten.

- Say: East represents the element Fire and the life energy Vision
    1. Have everyone turn to the right, East.
    2. Pause and hold for a silent count of ten.
- Say: West represents the element Water and the life energy Wisdom.
    1. Have everyone face in the direction the wand is pointing to, North.
    2. Pause and hold for a silent count of ten.
- Say: Turn your attention back to the center of the circle.
7. The facilitator explains that now, one at a time, they are to walk to the center of the circle, pick up the wand and share a personal value or belief with the group followed by an action that demonstrates that value or belief to the learning community. Here are some examples:
    - **I value** family. **As a teacher, I can demonstrate this by** making sure I communicate with parents once a week.
    - **I believe** that every child is special. **As a leader, I can demonstrate this by** dedicating a bulletin board on the first floor to recognize one student each week.
    - **I value** cleanliness. **As an administrator, I can** walk around the school during lunchtime to make sure all the hallways and bathrooms are clean and tidy.
    - **I believe** that teachers from diverse backgrounds are strong role models for students. **As a professor, I can** get involved in the hiring and search committee to see if we can find creative ways to recruit faculty from diverse backgrounds.
8. After everyone in the circle speaks, the facilitator should ask the group to contemplate the statements and think of one that stands out. Set the timer for 2 min.
9. When the timer goes off, go around the circle and have each one share one value or belief and an action from someone else in the group that they appreciated. For example,
    - **I appreciated when** Samantha talked about her value of family and how she is going to demonstrate this by communicating with parents once a week.

10. When everyone has had a turn, the facilitator should end the ritual by thanking the group for their participation.
    - The facilitator may want to point out in closure that one way we build trust is to align our words to actions and by making commitments to do this work within the community.
11. Individually reflect and write. Set the timer for 7 min.
    - How did engaging in this ritual make you feel?
    - What elements of the ritual did you appreciate?
    - What made you feel uncomfortable?
    - How might you have changed this ritual to make it a better experience?

2. Observing Rituals for Values

Purpose: To identify how rituals or ceremonies communicate certain values and beliefs

Overview: Participants observe and analyze elements of a ritual or ceremony

- ◆ You will need a notepad and a pencil/pen.
- ◆ Choose a ritual, ceremony or meeting to observe.
    - A ritual may involve one or more people. A ritual is a routine that has a deeper meaning. Putting a child to bed can be a ritual or a routine depending on the attention, care and inner processes involved. Example rituals include an artist getting ready to paint or an actor getting ready to perform; a morning meeting in a classroom; an opening of a school building; a healing, prayer or meditation; a housewarming; a dating ritual; or a holiday, birthday or dinner ritual.
    - Ceremonies are more formal. They include weddings, anniversaries, religious ceremonies, inductions, confirmations, completions, military ceremonies, club ceremonies, graduation.
    - If you choose to observe a meeting, it should be a regularly attended meeting, such as a PTA meeting, a union meeting or a faculty meeting.

- ◆ Before the observation, divide your paper into three columns and label: the first column, Actions and Language; the second column, Special Objects or Effects; and the last column, Values and Beliefs.
- ◆ Before entering the event, set some time aside to meditate for 5–10 min. (See Instructions for Meditation.)
- ◆ Bring to mind the three techniques for Transcensory Observation.
  - • Setting Intention;
  - • Bearing Witness;
  - • Suspending Judgment.
- ◆ Set the Intention: Insight.
  - • Remember, an intention directs your attention and energy to an outcome. The outcome is typically a disposition, virtue or state of being.
- ◆ Observe the entire ritual, ceremony or meeting while taking notes on your chart, filling in the first two columns only. Leave the Values and Beliefs column blank.
  - • Make sure you capture concrete behaviors and specific language.
  - • You may want to jot down who is in attendance and the role they play in the proceedings.
- ◆ Afterward, individually reflect on your list. Now, finish the last column thinking about what values or beliefs were demon-strated by the behaviors, language or manipulation of objects and effects.
- ◆ When the chart is filled in, review and contemplate the follow-ing questions individually in writing or discuss with a partner:
  - • What connections did you make between certain actions, behaviors, language, objects and values and beliefs?
  - • What emotions were displayed? What elements of the ritual do you think led to these emotions?
  - • Who appeared authentic and present? How do you know?
  - • How did levels of engagement change throughout the proceedings?
  - • What did you notice that surprised or confused you?
  - • If there was one thing that you would change to improve this ritual, ceremony or meeting, what would it be? Explain.

Connecting Strategy to Disposition

Inclusive

♦ How does a ceremony or ritual make each person feel a sense of belonging?

♦ In what ways can a ritual or ceremony be exclusive?

♦ How can we decline to engage in a ritual or ceremony in a way that promotes learning and transformation?

Strategy 3. Balanced Technology

Due to advancements in technology, people are reaching out to people all across the globe rooted in mutual interests and a passion for social change.[9]

One day in the middle of the busy school year, I had to travel to three different school sites to support six different teacher mentors, all before three o'clock. By the time I arrived at the third school, I was drained. I charged past the line of boisterous students and walked up three flights of stairs to meet my client. When I arrived, I was ushered into a small library. While I waited, I took out my laptop and logged onto our company's online platform. We were expected to capture evidence of every coaching conversation. The new system was great, but it was still fairly unpredictable in schools. The teacher arrived 10 minutes late, harried and pale. She had an armload of papers. I smiled and told her to sit down. Then, I went back to my screen, trying to troubleshoot a pesky pop-up window. When I looked up, the young teacher was crying. Between sobs, she apologized. She explained that she was overwhelmed. She had just found out that she had to cover for a sick teacher, and her own students were lagging behind. To make matters worse, she was scheduled for an evaluation at the end of the week. I peered over the top of my laptop at the girl's swollen eyes, and I was transported back to my first year of teaching. I took a deep breath, closed the lid on my computer and leaned in.

Technology and social media are the new power tools for learning, sharing information and building relationships. They are useful and convenient and move us beyond the four walls of the classroom. The internet is also the easiest way to connect and satisfy our boundless curiosity. Through the windows of cyberspace, we can catch a glimpse into the lives of others and interact with people over long distances. Technology is changing patterns of social interaction, communication and how we learn. We no longer feel limited by geography and we have access to information, world events and people that were previously off-limits. This open space produces feelings of freedom and agency.

However, as we observe and examine emerging patterns of behavior, we are learning how technology impacts our beliefs and values, our sense of self and possibility, what we think is real and important. With such a far-reaching influence, there is concern about how learning networks and internet platforms can be used as instruments by which institutions and corporations superimpose protocols, structures and criteria for success.[10] There is also evidence of internet and social media addiction, cyber-bullying, feelings of isolation and depression, increased anxiety and stress—all related to how we use technology. These problems raise important questions. When we think about Balanced Technology, we are thinking about how technology impacts our thoughts and beliefs, the quality of our social interactions, our ability to adapt to social situations and be responsive to individuals.

Activities

1. Cultivating Relationships in Cyber Space

Purpose: To demonstrate the opportunities and challenges of using the internet and social media for information and communication

Overview: Participants explore a research topic using technology

◆ You will need access to a computer, an internet connection and a social media platform such as Twitter, and a partner.

◆ Read the scenarios on the next page. Reflect on the situation and think about the opportunities and challenges related to technology, social media or the internet. Use the following prompts to guide your reflection:
- Who is involved and what happened?
- How was technology, the internet or social media involved?
- How did technology, the internet or social media create a problem or challenge?
- How did technology, the internet or social media create an opportunity?

◆ Choose one scenario to explore further. This scenario will be the basis for an inquiry you will conduct using a social media platform. Think about what we can learn from this scenario in order to leverage opportunities and mitigate the challenges.

◆ Formulate a question to focus your inquiry that combines the main topic of technology/internet/social media with a subtopic.
- Think about the keywords, terms, categories or hashtags you would use.
- Here are a few examples related to the scenarios:
  1. What are the **social and emotional skills** kids need for a board game that they can't learn from playing video games?
  2. How might technology create a barrier to **effective leadership and communication** in schools?
  3. How can technology interfere in effective **coaching and mentoring**?
  4. How can we harness young people's interest in social media to increase **student engagement** in school?
  5. How can we **assess internet sources** and identify developmentally appropriate and **culturally relevant material** for students?

◆ Now, prepare to host a Twitter chat on the topic.
- Log onto Twitter and see if you can join an existing chat so you can get the hang of the format.
- Choose your own hashtag.
- Set a convenient date and time frame for educators, typically 1 hour in duration.

- • Prepare four to five driving questions related to the discussion topic.
- • Create a simple but compelling announcement to promote your chat.
- ◆ Host the chat. Make sure you capture evidence of your learning.
  - • How many people participated?
  - • What question drew the most interesting responses?
  - • What response did you find the most surprising?
  - • What important information or resources did you come away with?
  - • What questions do you still have?
- ◆ Now, take the time to reflect on the experience individually or with a partner
  - • What benefits did you experience from this type of engagement?
  - • What challenges did you encounter?
  - • What did you notice about the participants and the interaction?
  - • In what ways does the chat format open up or close down a discussion, and how are they different from face-to-face communication?
  - • What patterns in the responses did you notice?
  - • Did you meet someone through the chat that you would want to follow or stay in touch with? Why or why not?

2. Learning from Direct Human Interaction

Purpose: To demonstrate the opportunities and challenges of using the internet and social media for communication and information

Overview: Participants explore a research topic without using technology

- ◆ You will need a pencil/pen and a notepad.
- ◆ Read the scenarios on the next page. Reflect on the situation and think about the opportunities and challenges related to technology, social media or the internet. Use the following prompts to guide your reflection:
  - • Who is involved and what happened?
  - • How was technology, the internet or social media involved?

- How did technology, the internet or social media create a problem or challenge?
- How did technology, the internet or social media create an opportunity?

◆ Choose a new scenario to explore. This scenario will be the basis for an inquiry you will conduct by interviewing people in the school community. Think about what we can learn from this scenario in order to leverage opportunities and mitigate the challenges?

◆ Formulate a driving question to focus your inquiry that combines the main topic of technology/internet/social media with a subtopic.

- Think about how you would frame the question.
- Here are a few examples related to the scenarios:
  1. What are the **social and emotional skills** kids need for a board game that they can't learn from playing video games?
  2. How might technology create a barrier to **effective leadership and communication** in schools?
  3. How can technology interfere in effective **coaching and mentoring**?
  4. How can we harness young people's interest in social media to increase **student engagement** in school?
  5. How can we **assess internet sources** and identify developmentally appropriate and **culturally relevant material** for students?

◆ Now, prepare to conduct Interviews. You will need to

- Choose four to five people in your school community whom you will invite to participate in the interview. Include a member of the faculty, administration, student body, parents and staff.
- Set a convenient date and time to meet with each individual. Expect the interview to last about 20–30 min.
- Prepare four to five driving questions related to the discussion topic.

◆ Conduct the interviews. Make sure you capture the answers in your notepad.

♦ When you have completed all the interviews, read through your data and consider the following:

- What question drew the most interesting responses?
- What response did you find the most surprising?
- What important information or resources did you come away with?
- What questions do you still have?

♦ Now, take the time to reflect on the experience individually or with a partner

- What benefits did you experience from this type of engagement?
- What challenges did you encounter?
- What did you notice about the participants and the nature of the interaction?
- In what way does the interview format open up or close down a discussion differently from online communication?
- What patterns in the responses did you notice?
- Did you meet someone through this experience that you would want to follow up with or stay in touch with? Why or why not?

Scenarios

1. At the last minute, Mr. Giovanni, an eighth-grade teacher, is stuck supervising a group of four students at lunchtime. He tells them to play a board game. Within 15 min, there is bickering and teasing, and one restless student keeps pushing hard on his chair, trying to balance his weight on the two back legs. Fearful that the situation will escalate, or the boy might get hurt, the teacher packs up the game and tells them to choose a book from the library. The restless student refuses to read, walks defiantly over to the computer station and searches for his favorite video game.

2. Mrs. Martinez, a veteran principal who has positive relationships in the community, struggles to keep up with the flow of over 500 emails monthly. She complains that email is eating up all of her time and preventing her from visiting classrooms and speaking with parents. In her inbox, there are several important messages

that go unread. A few teachers have begun to text her hoping to get her attention. The principal turns off the sound to her phone. If it is that important, she mutters, they'll make an appointment to meet me in person.

3. Dr. Wong, the instructional coach, scurries up three flights of the narrow school staircase to meet up with the newest teacher. She takes a seat and quickly pulls out her laptop, thinking she's only got 30 min before an important meeting with the Instructional Leadership Team. She says hello, while she logs onto the online platform. She goes through several screens, troubleshoots a few pop-up windows and prepares her document to take copious notes. By the time she looks up, the young teacher's face is covered in tears. Between sobs, she apologizes for wasting the coach's time, continuing on to say that an angry parent berated her in front of the students that morning, and she is now not sure she wants to continue teaching.

4. Gabe and Niko are best friends and attend the same high school. They both like the same girl, Samantha. After a huge fight with Gabe, Niko decides to ask Samantha out on social media. When Gabe sees the news, he is furious. To retaliate, he posts a picture of Samantha from summer camp where she is shown kissing a guy in front of the lake in a bathing suit. The post goes viral, and word spreads throughout the school that Samantha is loose. Horrified, Samantha tells her parents, who go straight to the principal's office and threaten to call the police on the grounds of slander and cyberbullying.

5. Ms. Francis is a fourth-grade teacher who has been teaching for 7 years. She always has her class under control and her test scores are top notch. She is consistently rated a highly effective teacher. There are a few English Language Learners (ELL) in her room that she is struggling with. They rarely speak up in class and it is hard for her to assess their understanding of the material. After attending a conference on culturally relevant pedagogy, she decides to teach a lesson on immigration, hoping that the topic will motivate this ELL group. She searches the internet, brings in several short stories and poems on the topic, and distributes them to her students. When she opens up the class for discussion, she notices that not one of the ELLs raises their hand to participate.

Connecting Strategy to Disposition

Responsive

- ♦ In what ways does technology influence our ability to be responsive to others?
- ♦ How do we know the best way to communicate with an individual?
- ♦ How can we assess whether our use of technology and the internet is balanced?

Strategy 4. Bearing Witness

> It was the behavior of a child that suffered from neglect, an unstable home environment, and perhaps other influences of which I was not aware.[11]

I am thinking about a conversation I had with a school transformation specialist. She was describing her doctoral research and trips to Africa. "If you saw the conditions over there," she said, "you wouldn't think black people in America have it that bad." I am thinking about my partner at an anti-racist training who tells me that her South African father had black servants but is not racist because he didn't beat them. I am thinking about the caravan of migrants traveling from Honduras to the Mexico-US border, who are either "largely men, young and strong, a lot of bad people and people that are in gangs" or "a bunch of impoverished, malnourished refugees a thousand miles away."[12] I am thinking about the 11 people killed in a synagogue and the shooting on the Gaza border. I am thinking about the Thai children and their coach trapped in a cave, the Puerto Rican mother without food or electricity reaching out to grab a roll of paper towels. I am thinking about the homeless man I pass while worrying how I will cover next month's rent and the 15,000 public school children sleeping in shelters when I tuck my daughter in. How can I possibly make sense of human suffering like this? How can I possibly know what I can do to make a difference?

Adversity takes us out of our comfort zone and reminds us what it means to be vulnerable. Sometimes adversity is a surprise, like the sudden loss of a job. Other times, it is endemic and indicative of an inequitable society. Regardless, any experience that creates the feeling of suffering influences our thoughts and behavior more than any professional training or formal study. As educators, we experience and witness different kinds of suffering every day. How do we pay attention to our own suffering and the suffering of others so that we are altered at the core, at the level of consciousness, so that we become a source for healing, justice and social responsibility?

According to Dr. Donald Pfaff, we are naturally good and biologically wired for altruism. He has found that contrary to common wisdom that human nature is essentially selfish, the human brain is actually programmed to care for others and to be kind. In other words, we are wired for goodwill. However, he explains, to act altruistically, one must picture the person who will be the target of their altruistic act in such a way that the image of that person blurs with the image of one's self, which provides the basis for treating the other like oneself.[13]

Bearing witness is acknowledging that an experience is real and true because we know it exists in one form or another as shared human experience. When we position ourselves outside experience, as if we are independent of it, we are creating a barrier between us and truth, which limits our ability to respond with compassion. Bearing witness involves being with, blending into, blurring oneself with and becoming "a part of" another person's experience.

When we bear witness to suffering, it is much more difficult. Suffering repels us. How is this possible we say? We want to close our eyes; we don't want any part of it. This is especially true when the suffering is the result of physical and emotional abuse or atrocities inflicted in time of war, hate or mental illness. We don't want to see and feel that pain. We are ashamed to be a part of the human race.

In response to this, Aurora Levins Morales, Puerto Rican Jewish writer, teacher and activist writes,

What is so dreadful is that to transform the traumatic, we must re-enter it fully, and allow the full weight of grief to pass through our hearts. It is not possible to digest atrocity without tasting it first, without assessing it on our tongues, the full bitterness of it. Through mourning everything we have lost, we discover that we have in fact survived, that our spirits are indestructible.[14]

Activities

1. Castaway

Purpose: To gain insight into the nature of suffering and to identify skills that promote healing, resilience and change

Overview: Participants think about a difficult, painful or adverse experience in their life and share important details with a compassionate listener

- ◆ You will need a partner and a timer.
- ◆ Each person should bring to mind a difficult, painful or adverse experience.
  - Some examples are the loss of a loved one, loss of a job or getting fired, separation or divorce, financial hardship, an illness or serious accident, labor and childbirth, and failing an important examination.
- ◆ As you think about your experience, refer to the following questions:
  - What happened?
  - Who was involved?
  - How did you feel?
  - How would you describe your behavior during that time?
  - Have you recovered from the experience?
  - What has changed since then?
- ◆ Take a few minutes to contemplate what happened to you. Set the intention: Empathy. Set the timer for 3 min.
- ◆ Choose who will speak first and who will be the Compassionate Listener.

- The speaker starts by sharing the experience. The Compassionate Listener practices Deep Listening. Set the timer for 7 min.
  - Practice Deep Listening Skills
    1. Listen for thoughts and use of language.
    2. Listen for feelings and relationships.
    3. Listen for insight and emerging ideas.
- When the speaker has finished, the Compassionate Listener can now ask clarifying questions using the questions above as a guide.
- To conclude, the Compassionate Listener and the speaker discuss the following questions together:
  - What can we learn from this experience?
  - What kind of people do we rely on when faced with difficult situations?
  - What could we have done differently?
- Now, switch. The speaker becomes the Compassionate Listener.

2. Mapping a Spiritual Journey

Purpose: To learn important skills and dispositions from individuals who have participated in or led human rights movements

Overview: Participants will select a human rights leader or activist and map out how the spirit of the character changed over time

- You need a group of three to four people, access to a computer with internet connection, chart paper, markers and a timer.
- The group selects one human rights leader, civil rights leader or activist.
  - A human rights leader is a person that figures prominently in a group's efforts to attain freedom, equal rights or justice.
  - An activist is a person who engages in activities to promote social change.
  - Examples of leaders are Mahatma Gandhi, Eleanor Roosevelt, Cesar Chaves, Martin Luther King, Jr., Nelson Mandela, Mother Teresa, Malcolm X, Ellie Wiesel, Gloria Steinem, Mary Yuriko.
- As a group, read through the questions that will guide the investigation:

- What period of history and geographical location is associated with this person?
- What is the injustice that this person worked to change?
- What significant details characterize this person's early life?
- What life event/s revealed injustice?
- What inspired this person to champion for change?
- What challenges or struggles did this person face?
- What did this person do to inspire others?
- What strategies did this person use to change society?

◆ Engage in independent research using the internet or by accessing books and resources made available. Set the timer for 25 min.
  - The group may choose to divide up the research questions to maximize time.

◆ Write the person's name on the top in bold letters. Draw a timeline stretching from one end of the page to another at the center.

◆ Set the intention: Agency. Allow the group to contemplate for a few minutes on Agency. Set the timer to 3 min.
  - Agency is the belief that through one's effort, we can make a difference in the world.

◆ Now, have each person share important key events from their investigation to add to the top of the timeline. Add dates to show sequence. Set the timer for 10 min.

◆ As a group, consider each event and match each event with a disposition or barrier that you believe can be associated with each juncture of the leader's journey. Use the chart below. Set timer for 10 min.

Dispositions	Reflective	Trustworthy	Creative
	Focused	Inclusive	Wise
	Self-Assured	Responsive	Curious
	Inspiring	Compassionate	Powerful
Barriers	Impatience	Guilt	Cynicism
	Stress	Isolation	Egotism
	Hypocrisy	Rigidity	Complacency
	Fear	Shame	Fatigue

- When the chart is complete, take a few minutes to appreciate the results. Set the timer to 2 min.
- Share with others.

Connecting Strategy to Disposition

Compassionate

- How can paying attention to our own suffering support our ability to be compassionate?
- How can we better understand the impact of chronic adversity and suffering?
- What deters us from being compassionate in our professional practice?
- How can we teach and encourage compassion in others?

Assessing for Barriers

The two greatest barriers to the realization of freedom are considering another person's freedom a threat to our own safety and security and keeping us from freedom through abstraction. Both are a consequence of the mind, a lack of trust and fear. We talk about freedom but rarely do we stop to examine what we mean, what it looks like and how it applies to each individual.

The mind is a process that regulates the flow of energy and information.[15] If your mind is cluttered or concerned with threats (real or imaginary), it will hamper the flow of energy needed to see things clearly. When you shift the focus of your mind to your power and purpose, and the joy it gives you, you begin to channel the flow of energy and information to this area. You will begin to see how freedom applies to your immediate context. If your power and purpose is in the field of education, for example, don't get lost in freedom out there, in some distant location; consider what it means to cultivate freedom in the classroom, in relationships with students, parents, staff, teachers and so on. If your power and purpose is in the health profession, consider freedom in your interactions with patients or how you might challenge unfair power dynamics in health care management. It is easy to get distracted and discouraged, until we invite freedom into ordinary situations. So, remember you are either magical, or you are not. Ask yourself, what does freedom look like in this moment, in this situation?

Organizational Trust

Research in neuroscience led by Dr. Paul J. Zak, has led to the discovery that levels of oxytocin in the brain is correlated to trust. The brain's production of oxytocin, combined with its effects on the central and peripheral nervous systems, motivates voluntary cooperation. Oxytocin makes it feel good to cooperate with others by increasing awareness of other's emotional states and increasing prosocial behaviors by enhancing the subjective experience of empathy.[16] By testing for levels of oxytocin in response to various stimuli, Zak found that we can increase trust in groups by publicly recognizing excellence, providing the team with an attainable challenge, giving choice in tasks, being transparent and open with information, and cultivating caring social bonds.[17]

Activity

Take a moment to think about the learning and activities from this chapter and fill out this chart to consider barriers to Freedom and next steps. Again, this is not an exhaustive list. Trust yourself and your feelings as you process your learning and use the example for guidance.

Strategies	Potential Barrier/s	Next Steps
Intergroup Dialogue	Example: Distrust	Example: Before getting into a group scenario, find a person from a different background or with different beliefs and values to engage in a courageous conversation

Strategies	Potential Barrier/s	Next Steps
Rituals and Ceremony		
Balanced Technology		
Bearing Witness		

Application to Practice: Observation Tool

The following is an *Observation Tool* to help you observe and assess for Freedom. All three domains involve contemplative practices, discoveries, dispositions and awareness that are nonlinear and subtle. For this reason, the use of tools or instruments for planning, observation or assessment should be considered entry points for discussion and analysis.

Freedom Observation Tool

Strategies	Teacher Behaviors	Student Behaviors
Intergroup Dialogue	• Arranges space and time for dialogue • Communicates value and purpose for dialogue • Engages participants of diverse backgrounds whenever possible • Reviews Conscientious Engagement Norms • Connects dialogue to prior learning and other relevant topics • Provides resources or materials • Models freedom dispositions • Frames the dialogue using questions related to culture, identity, social issues and justice • Helps clarify terms and definitions • Documents and summarizes ideas for group • Provides reflection and metacognition activities	• Engages in dialogue • Follows Conscientious Engagement Norms and suggests alternative norms for optimal engagement • Examines resources and makes connections • Asks questions • Practices freedom dispositions • Engages in reflection and metacognition activities • Demonstrates willingness to practice facilitation techniques and lead dialogue
Rituals and Ceremony	• Incorporates ritual and ceremony to build trust and community • Provides opportunities to explore rituals and ceremonies from a variety of cultures • Encourages new rituals and ceremonies • Prepares alternative activities for students who choose to disengage in ways that promote learning and healing	• Participates in rituals and ceremonies to build trust and community • Explores rituals and ceremonies from a variety of cultures • Self-monitors level of engagement • Proposes new rituals and ceremonies • Practices disengaging in ways that promote learning and healing, and accepts alternative activities
Balanced Technology	• Plans for Balanced Technology • Models how technology and social media can open up learning opportunities • Communicates and anticipates challenges related to technology and social • Provides equal opportunities to conduct online research and face-to-face research	• Takes a reflective stance about the use of technology • Uses technology and social media to explore learning opportunities • Anticipates challenges related to technology and social media and seeks guidance and support • Practices online research and face-to-face research

Strategies	Teacher Behaviors	Student Behaviors
	• Identifies the social and emotional skills for building authentic social networks	• Practices the social and emotional skills for building authentic social networks
Bearing Witness	• Creates opportunities for storytelling • Models and encourages deep listening • Integrates human rights movements and civil rights history • Helps identify historical texts and resources • Designs creative activities to make meaningful connections between historical events and character development	• Shares personal lived experiences • Practices deep listening • Studies human rights movements and civil rights history • Examines historical texts and resources • Makes meaningful connections between historical events and character development

Checking In

Go back to your Initial Self-Assessment. Review your answers to Part II. Freedom. Reflect on the following questions:

- ◆ What are three things you learned about the practice of Freedom?
- ◆ Why is Social Awareness and Adaptability important in your practice?
- ◆ What aspect of this domain do you want to concentrate on moving forward?
- ◆ How can we create a safe space to explore complex social issues with colleagues?
- ◆ What questions do you still have?

Notes

1 Rios, R. (2017) *Teacher Agency for Equity: A Framework for Conscientious Engagement*. Routledge, New York, p. 156.
2 Rios, R. The Weight and Weightlessness of Courageous Conversations. December 2, 2017 Conscientious Engagement

Blog. Retrieved from https://conscientiousengagement.com/
2017/12/02/the-weight-or-weightlessness-of-courageous-
conversations/

3   Sanchez-Flores, M.J. (2017) Mindfulness and Complex Identities in
    Equity Training: A Pilot Study. *European Review of Applied Sociol-*
    ogy, Vol. 10, No. 14, p. 25.

4   Scharmer, O. and Peter Senge's work on Presencing. (2014)
    Connecting Inner Transformation as a Leader to Corporate and
    Societal Change. *Leading with Spirit, Presence, & Authenticity*,
    Edited by K.G. Schuyler, Jossey-Bass, San Francisco, CA,
    pp. 32–33.

5   Senge, P., Scharmer, C.O., Jaworski, J. and Flowers, B.S. (2004)
    Presence: Human Purpose and the Field of the Future, Crown
    Publishing, New York, p. 86.

6   Rios, R. (2017) *Teacher Agency for Equity: A Framework for*
    Conscientious Engagement. Routledge, New York, p. 162.

7   Zak, P.J. (2017) The Neuroscience of Trust. *Harvard Business Review*,
    January–February Issue. Retrieved from https://hbr.org/2017/01/
    the-neuroscience-of-trust

8   Arrien, A. (1993) The Four-Fold Way: Walking the Paths of the
    Warrior, Teacher, Healer and Visionary, Harper One, Harper Collins
    Publishing, New York

9   Rios, R. (2017) *Teacher Agency for Equity: A Framework for*
    Conscientious Engagement. Routledge, New York, p. 161.

10 Frankham, J. (2006) Network Utopias and Alternative Entangle-
    ments for Educational Research and Practice. *Journal of Education*
    Policy, Vol. 21, No. 6, pp. 661–677.

11 Rios, R. (2017) Teacher Agency for Equity: A Framework for
    Conscientious Engagement. Routledge, New York, p. 162.

12 Fox News, Trump on Key Midterm Races and Stop-
    ping the Caravan. Retrieved from https://video.foxnews.
    com/v/5855096286001/?#sp=show-clips

13 Pfaff, D.W. (2015) *The Altruistic Brain: How We Are Naturally Good*.
    Oxford University Press, New York, pp. 4–11.

14 Levins Morales, A. (1998) *Medicine Stories: History, Culture*
    and the Politics of Integrity. South End Press, Cambridge,
    MA, p. 19.

15   Siegel, D. (2007) *The Mindful Brain*, Mind Your Brain, W. W. Norton & Company Inc., New York & London, p. 5.

16   Zak, P.J. (2018) The Neuroscience of High Trust Organizations, *Consulting Psychology Journal: Practice and Research*, Vol. 70, No. 1, pp. 46–47.

17   Zak, P.J. (2017) The Neuroscience of Trust, *Harvard Business Review*, January–February. Retrieved from https://hbr.org/2017/01/the-neuroscience-of-trust

5

Emergence

Transpersonal Awareness and Agency

The willingness to reposition ourselves outside the center of action redistributes power and breaks down notions of ethnocentrism in ways that ensure the vision and driver of action lies within the people themselves.[1]

Throughout history, we have seen how through human effort, we can imagine and build a better world. Emergence is the ability to channel energy in ways that facilitate the integration of new ideas for equity. Ideas that can help us reduce suffering and improve the quality of life have value. When we look to wisdom traditions, advancements in science and human rights movements, we can identify ideas and strategies that are aligned to a higher purpose and worthy of our attention and effort. Envisioning a future that has not come to pass and taking responsibility for moving us into that future require us to access the parts of our brain responsible for creativity and novel thinking as well as a deep understanding of the invisible forces that move people to action. With imagination and creativity, and a refined attention to our individual and collective energy, we can identify valuable new ideas and strategically weave them into our work for personal and social transformation. Transpersonal Awareness and Agency lead to Emergence. In this chapter, we explore four strategies associated with Emergence, engage in activities, reflect on experience and think about how to apply Emergence to practice.

The following are dispositions and barriers associated with Emergence to be recognized and anticipated. At the end of each strategy, you will be prompted to think about a disposition to process your learning. At the end of the chapter, you will have the opportunity to synthesize your experience, consider barriers and apply to practice.

Dispositions

Creative: Originality in thought and expression; the ability to produce and manifest an idea into reality;

Wise: Having knowledge, insight and discernment;

Compassionate: The willingness to listen deeply and bear witness to the suffering of others and to help relieve that suffering;

Powerful: The ability to influence people and situations.

Barriers

Cynicism: Distrust and skepticism; believing that people are motivated by self-interest;

Egotism: Excessive focus and emphasis on one's self and one's importance;

Complacency: Self-satisfaction, security or comfort in the way things are without the awareness or willingness to consider possible vulnerabilities, flaws or injustices in the existing conditions;

Fatigue: The lack of energy; feeling drained and tired.

Strategy 1. Envisioning and Imagination

A few years ago, when facilitating a professional learning session for instructional coaches in a large school district, we hit a brick wall in the middle of an activity. The topic was *Schools We Envision*. At first, there was a surge of enthusiasm, but midway through, we noticed a lull in energy. We walked around to observe and listen. We heard participants say: What does it matter what we envision? We don't have the power to change anything. Do these guys know how things work around here? This is a waste of time. My colleague and I got into a huddle to plan. There were several more steps left to the activity, but if the coaches did not see the purpose, what was the point of continuing? My colleague, who had strong relationships in the district, explained that the coaches were spread thin. They were tired and kept on a tight leash. Several visionary leaders had recently left the district frustrated. "This activity might feel too unrealistic and disconnected from their reality," she explained. When we left the training that day, we were lost in thought. How can we shift a group out of that feeling of powerlessness? How can we transport educators into that space where magic, hope, dreams and superpowers live?

When I returned home, I paced my living room. The oil painting I had just finished shimmered in the distance. Next to my easel was my favorite art book. I walked over, picked it up and turned to the page with a purple sticky note. This is what it read:

> The slightly altered consciousness state of feeling transported, which most artists experience while drawing, painting, sculpting, or doing any kind of art work, is a state probably not altogether unfamiliar to you. You may have observed slight shifts in your state of consciousness while engaging in much more ordinary activities than artwork. For example, most people are aware that they occasionally slip from ordinary waking consciousness into the slightly altered state of daydreaming. As another example, people often say that reading takes them "out of themselves." And other kinds of activities which apparently produce a shift in consciousness are meditation, jogging, needlework, typing, listening to music, and of course, drawing itself.[2]

I continued to read well into the night. The answers I was searching for were right there. The right side of the brain is the visual, perceptual mode of the brain. It is nonverbal, holistic, visuospatial. In the right hemisphere mode of information processing, we also use our intuition, resulting in leaps of insight.[3] Using the right side of the brain also typically makes us feel like time is passing without noticing. It is not surprising that it is this right side that is most active in children in the first 2 or 3 years. On the other hand, the left side of the brain specializes in linguistics, linearity, logic and literal thinking.[4] Most schooling experience emphasizes language and left-brain activities which ends up feeling like the norm.

In order for us to evolve and transform our schools and society, we need to invest more of our time cultivating imagination and constructing learning experiences where artists and intellectuals are born, where creativity thrives, and where visionaries teach and lead. We need to be deliberate about shifting into the right-brain mode and get comfortable and confident in that space. One way to do this is to integrate image-based explorations. What are we working towards? What do we see?

Activities

1. Right Side, Upside Down[5]

Purpose: To engage in an image-based exploration to shift into right-brain mode

Overview: Participants draw an image from memory, and copy a partner's image that is turned upside down

- ◆ You will need a large sheet of paper, markers or a charcoal pencil, a timer and a partner.
- ◆ Decide what each person will draw.
  - A school campus;
  - A classroom;
  - A famous person;
  - A neighborhood.
- ◆ Close your eyes and bring the image of a real school, classroom, neighborhood or famous person to mind. Set the timer for 2 min.
  - Choose a location or person you are familiar with.
  - Visualize as many details as possible.

- Now, take a piece of chart paper and draw the image from memory. Do not let your partner see your drawing. Set the timer for 8 min.
  - Capture as many details as possible.
  - Stay present and aware of the experience.
- When your drawing is complete, take it and hang it upside down on a nearby wall or flat surface. Now, switch places with your partner so that you are facing their upside-down drawing. Take a new sheet of paper and your writing tool and copy the drawing. Set the timer for 8 min.
  - Do not turn the drawing right side up at any time.
  - Start from any point, keep 1–2 feet away from the picture.
  - Capture as many details as possible, follow the lines.
  - Stay present and aware of your experience.
- When the drawings are complete, turn the originals rights side up and hang the copies side by side. Arrange so they are easy to see.
- Stand in front of the results and inspect the artwork. Set the timer for 2 min.
- Reflect on the experience individually in writing or with your partner:
  - Where the results what you expected? Why or why not?
  - Where you able to copy accurately even from an upside-down model?
  - Which drawing felt harder or more challenging? Why?
  - Which drawing made you feel more confident?
  - Which drawing absorbed your attention more?
  - Which drawing did you enjoy more? Why?

2. Crystal Balls[6]

- You will need chart paper, markers, a timer and a group of three to five people.
- Choose one idea that you believe would make a big difference for schools or society. Consider the following examples or come up with one as a group:
  - School
    1. Smaller class sizes;
    2. Higher teacher salaries;

       3. A more diverse teacher workforce;
       4. Alternative Assessments;
       5. Yoga.
- Society
  1. Affordable housing;
  2. Green space;
  3. Universal health care;
  4. High-quality supermarkets in every neighborhood;
  5. Renewable energy.

◆ After the decision has been made, one person in the group should draw a circle at the center of the chart paper and write the big idea inside.

◆ Now, set the intention: Insight
- An intention directs your attention and energy to an outcome. The outcome is typically a disposition, virtue or state of being.
- Sometimes, we connect an intention to a particular problem we want to solve, such as how to resolve a conflict with a student, boss or colleague. An intention of this nature would take the form of a statement such as "Using insight in order to visualize how things might be better at school."

◆ Take a few minutes to visualize the big idea. Set the timer for 3 min.
- What would it look like if it this big idea were a reality?
- How would it impact people and the environment?

◆ Choose one person to write/draw for the group.

◆ Starting from the center and working outward, draw four circles surrounding the inner circle.

◆ Then the group should discuss possible positive outcomes or consequences as a result of the big idea and possible negative consequences or outcomes as a result of the big idea. (See Figure 5.1.)
- Each person should share the possibilities in visual terms. For example, if the big idea is a School Library, members of the group might say,
  1. I see teachers walking to the library with their students.
  2. I see students stealing the new books from the library.

FIGURE 5.1 Crystalizing the Future.

- ◆ As the ideas emerge, the writer should capture them into the bubbles.
  - • Afterward, go outward to the next layer, and do the same, attaching positive and negative outcomes or consequence to that layer of circles. For example,
    1. I see students playing around in the halls.
    2. I see students reading more.
- ◆ Continue the process. Set the timer for 8 min.
- ◆ When the crystal balls are complete, stand back and quietly contemplate the experience. Set the timer for 2 min.

♦ Individually write or discuss the following:
  • Were there any imagined outcomes that surprised you?
  • What were the outcomes that might make others feel uncomfortable or apprehensive? How might you respond to their concerns?
  • Do all ideas have positive and negative outcomes? Why or why not?
  • How do you feel about the big idea at the center after engaging in this activity?

Connecting Strategy to Disposition

Creative

1. What are the benefits of engaging in creative activities at work?
2. In what ways have you been creative in your practice?
3. How do others respond to creative individuals at work?
4. How might too much creativity be unproductive?

Strategy 2. Wisdom Traditions and Philosophy

> These limits prevent us from exploring ways to infuse education with integrative, holistic learning and creative spaces to raise non-religious consciousness about the nature of wisdom, truth, and divine intelligence.[7]

When teaching a course on teaching literacy through a collaborative study of social identity, I stood in front of the whiteboard and asked the students to pop-corn out universal values that they believe every human being would agree upon, regardless of religion, culture, language, gender, sexual orientation and so on. There was a long, awkward silence. Finally, one student spoke up. "It's not that easy. If we say something like, love or honesty, how do we know that everyone would agree on what those things actually mean?" I smiled and told her she had made an excellent point. Later, after our discussion, while reading through their reflections, I learned that many of the students were caught up by the word "universal." What does universal mean? Is there such thing as universal values, or a *universal* wisdom? If so, what is it? How do we describe it, talk about it and are we all talking about the same thing? Most importantly, why is this an important conversation to have right now, in the field of education? If there is no such thing as universal wisdom or a universal set of values, how are we to design an education system designed for the whole child—academically, socially, emotionally and spiritually?

According to Maslow, every human being has the same basic needs: survival, safety, love and belonging, self-esteem and self-fulfillment. It seems to me that these classifications are clues into understanding universal wisdom or universal values. Then, there is the Pathway to Transcendence, aligned to the chakras, explored in Chapter 3. Themes like survival and fear, love and openness, identity and power, compassion and self-acceptance, communication, truth, purpose and freedom are all there. Aren't these similar to Maslow's hierarchy? (See Figure 5.2.) What can we learn about universal wisdom from these two conceptual frames that organize human experience?

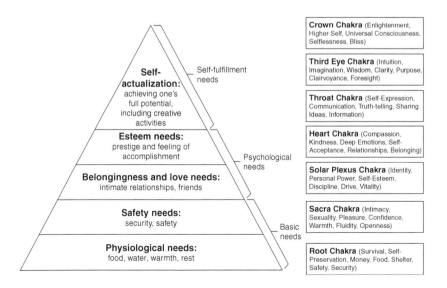

FIGURE 5.2 Comparing Maslow's Hierarchy to the Chakras.

To educate, from the Latin, educare, means to draw out. This implies that the process of education is to draw out knowledge that exists within, rather than from the outside. Is there some universal wisdom or knowledge we have *inside* ourselves?

The strategy *Wisdom Traditions and Philosophy* is based on the premise that human beings will naturally gravitate to learning experiences that draw out knowledge from within, and that lead to wisdom. The term Wisdom Traditions is based on the idea that when we study all religious and spiritual traditions, we can identify common understandings, in other words, universal wisdom. Philosophy is the study of knowledge and a search for truth. It is a way of thinking by reasoning and contemplating problems that can lead us to understand the true nature of human experience, existence and reality. This strategy, therefore, involves learning to understand the true nature of self, and the purpose of existence by studying our own experience and knowledge passed down from generation to generation through oral and written traditions, knowledge that also lives inside of us by way of our membership to humanity, or collective consciousness. When we design learning experiences that respond to our inner drive to 'know thyself' and to become wise—that which is universal and transcendent—we naturally engage students.

The strategy Wisdom Traditions and Philosophy is about interrogating ideas, refining our thinking and considering questions of human significance and of a moral and ethical nature. It is only when we hold on to the illusion that there are infinite pathways and each has equal merit, that we are likely to repeat the same mistakes over and over.

Activities

1. Analyzing Texts for Deeper Meaning

Purpose: To analyze texts and engage in a Socratic Seminar in order to identify perennial themes

Overview: A group reads a text by John Dewey and a text by Martin Luther King, Jr., on the purpose of education and engages in a philosophical analysis and discussion of the text

♦ You will need a copy of the two texts, chart paper, a marker, a timer and a group of three to five participants.

    ● Read: *My Pedagogical Creed* by John Dewey http://dewey. pragmatism.org/creed.htm

    ● Read: The Purpose of Education by Martin Luther King, Jr. https://kinginstitute.stanford.edu/king-papers/documents/purpose-education

    ● Always choose a text that lends itself to philosophical discussion. This means a text that is open to interpretation and elucidates the complex nature of knowledge, values, existence and human experience.

♦ Each member of the group should have read the text selections twice before arriving and should have come up with one to two questions that spark genuine curiosity. Questions that drive philosophical discussions are

    ● Open-ended, with no right or wrong answer;

    ● Simply stated and meaningful to the group;

    ● Related to a topic of human significance.

♦ At the start of the discussion, read aloud the questions and choose one question for the discussion. Write it down on the chart paper, and make it visible to the whole group. Here are few examples:

    ● In what ways has the purpose of public education changed?

    ● Is it possible to work toward a shared moral compass in education? Why, or why not?

    ● What challenges do we face when we advocate for a moral and ethical basis for our practice in education?

♦ Reread the text selections and annotate, keeping the question in mind. Set the timer for 15 min.

    ● Underline important phrases.

    ● Circle key terms.

    ● Write notes in the margins or on sticky notes.

♦ Choose a facilitator for the discussion. The facilitator keeps the pace slow and deliberate, and stops to clarify terminology or unfamiliar words. The facilitator also encourages participants to

    ● Refer to the text to support ideas.

    ● Compare and contrast ideas from both authors.

- Ask follow-up questions and offer counterarguments.
- Paraphrase, summarize and extend thinking.
- Define Socratic seminar.
    - A dialectical conversation where participants seek to deepen their understanding of complex ideas in text rather than by memorizing.[8]
    - Socratic seminars have opening questions, core questions and closing questions
- Before starting the conversation, set the intention: Wisdom.
    - An intention directs your attention and energy to an outcome. The outcome is typically a disposition, virtue or state of being.
- Contemplate what it means to be wise. Set the timer for 3 min.
- Start the discussion. Set the timer for 25 min.
- At the end, silently contemplate the discussion and insights from the texts. Set the timer for 3 min.
- Individually reflect and write on the following questions.
    - How were the two points of view similar? How were they different?
    - What wisdom did you take away from this conversation?
- As a group, discuss
    - How did you feel engaging in this style of interaction?
    - How did your group manage any differences of opinion or text interpretation?
    - How did grounding the conversation in a text help the group understand the topic?

2. Ethical Culture

Purpose: To consider the role of ethics in the field of education and to practice a method by which we can learn from ethical dilemmas

Overview: Participants define values, consider real scenarios and problem solve together

- You will need a chart paper, Ethical Dilemma Scenarios, a marker, a timer and a group of three to six participants.
- Choose a facilitator who will take notes on the chart and manage time and the flow of the activity.

- On the chart paper, draw a T-Chart, label the left side Personal Values and the right side Organizational Values.
- Start by individually contemplating Personal Values. Set the timer for 3 min.
  - Personal Values refer to what is important to you, what you think is useful and worthy, and what you prioritize in life.
  - Examples include health, honesty, independence, family, money, education, vacation time, space and nature.
- Now, have each member share our Personal Values, while the facilitator captures on the chart.
- Repeat the same for Organizational Values. Contemplate Organizational Values. Set the timer for 3 min.
  - Organizational Values refer to what is important to an organization or company, what they think is useful and deserves merit or recognition, what they prioritize at all levels.
  - Organizational Values are often related to Institutional Values, which are values that are shared across several organizations in a system, such as a school district or a chain of providers in the health-care system.
  - Examples include positive attitude, willingness to work long hours, loyalty, compliance, collaboration, safety and credentials.
- Now, each member shares Organizational Values, while the facilitator captures them on the chart.
- When the chart is complete, take a few minutes to read and contemplate the two columns. Set the timer for 2 min.
- Discuss
  - How are the two sides similar? How are they different?
  - What values matter the most when approaching an ethical dilemma at work?
- Define Ethics. Inform the participants that they will be reading through ethical dilemmas and engaging in a protocol in order to practice moral reasoning.
  - Ethics is a code of values and moral principles; it concerns issues pertaining to conduct and character, evaluating what is right and wrong, what is the responsibility of a person and whether or not a person has free will to act in a situation.
- Distribute the Ethical Dilemma Scenarios. Individually read and take a few minutes to contemplate the dilemmas. Set the timer for 7 min.

- Think about Personal Values and Organizational Values.
- Think about how you might respond to each situation.
- As a group, choose one scenario to discuss. Read the scenario out loud. Each person goes around and comments on the scenario, focusing on the following questions:
  - How does the scenario align with your Personal Values?
  - How does the scenario align with our Organizational or Institutional Values?
- Take a moment to consider how to address the dilemma thinking about clashes between Personal and Organizational Values. Set the timer for 2 min.
- Now, each person takes a turn suggesting how to address the dilemma in one of three ways. Set the timer for 12 min.
  - Offer an alternative approach.
  - Present a solution.
  - Suggest a course of action.
- After everyone has had a turn, the facilitator should open the discussion to consider counterarguments. Set the timer for 8 min.
  - What negative consequences or outcomes may result from this alternative approach, solution or course of action?
- Conclude by individually writing a response to the following questions:
  - How did this discussion influence your thinking?
  - How can we respond wisely to ethical dilemmas without jeopardizing our job?
  - What strategies can we encourage others to use in order to respond wisely when faced with an ethical dilemma?

Connecting Strategy to Disposition

Wise

- How would you define wisdom?
- How can wisdom literature and philosophical discussions support our ability to make wise decisions?
- What other activities cultivate wisdom that can help us improve our practice?
- How can we support others to consider morality and ethics as it relates to their professional practice?

Ethical Dilemmas Scenarios

1. After a 6-month search for employment, a preservice teacher with student loans grapples with whether or not to accept a job offer to teach at an urban charter school that is known for its controversial discipline policies and mismanagement of money.

2. Tammy has been working for 8 years in a school district with the lowest teacher salaries in the nation. She is a single parent with two children, struggling to cover the bills. In response to gun violence and school shootings, her school district is piloting a program to put metal detectors in schools and train teachers to carry concealed weapons. Teachers who enter the program will receive student loan forgiveness and an increase in salary.

3. Gregory, an elementary school teacher, is working in a school where teachers are given monetary incentives for having the highest test scores. Teachers compete for the best students at the end of each year and do "test prep" 2 months in advance, at the expense of other subjects and creative activities. This time of year, students become anxious, stressed and bad-tempered.

4. As part of an integration plan in a large school district, the superintendent plans to change the criteria for a top performing, specialized high school that bases admission on the score from one exam. At present, the school is majority Asian, working- and middle-class families who travel from all over the city to attend. Parents are concerned that the quality of instruction and school reputation will be negatively impacted if they change the admissions criteria. Historically, families with means leave the public system, opt for private schools or move to surrounding suburban areas.

5. In a conservative school community, a secretly gay teacher struggles with how to create an inclusive school experience for gay, lesbian, bisexual and transgendered students who are being bullied.

6. A new teacher discovers that there are no ESL classes or bilingual programs, even though 70% of the students are English Language Learners, and 18% are facing homelessness. The staff is expected to work 60-hour weeks because of a lack of curriculum and support.

7. You are on a hiring committee for leadership positions. One of the goals is to increase diversity. At the first meeting, you learn that candidates are expected to complete a 4-hour-long performance task at an early stage of the process. Several experienced candidates from underrepresented groups have refused. You learn that asking for a performance task is a well-known strategy that organizations use to steal ideas and get work done without having to pay consulting fees.

Strategy 3. Shared Mindful Inquiry

> In spite of the wealth of knowledge and research we have on equity, we really don't have the answer to the dilemma we face.[9]

Being part of a national instructional design team was a dynamic learning experience. In order for us to design the best learning products for our clients, we had to channel our energy wisely and learn how to work together as a well-functioning team. When we first started, we experienced hiccups and growing pains. Our team was diverse, consisting of veteran writers and newbies, folks who lived in the Eastern, Pacific and Central time zones; each of us had a unique skill set, talent, culture, personality and professional aspirations. The hardest thing, we found, was developing a system and a protocol that was structured enough, but also flexible enough to support creativity. We wanted to harness talent and skill while maintaining a healthy flow of information and communication across the team. We discovered that we had to continuously clarify purpose and desired outcomes, identify which were the best ideas and what were the concrete steps to meet our goals. I realized throughout this experience how much we have evolved. We have evolved in lifestyle and living arrangements, our expectations about work, how we communicate and how we process information. It is no wonder organizations are struggling to keep up. We need time to reflect on these changes, to consider which norms are outdated. We need to spend quality time developing new structures and protocols for working together. We also need to establish ground rules for process based on a commitment to mindfulness, inquiry and equity.

As we move into the role of a Master Teacher, we will inevitably find that a big part of our job is advocating for new systems and protocols for professional learning, experimenting with new ways of doing and reflecting on experience in a way that leads to growth, knowledge and transformation. It is essential that we push back on the constraints on our time and make a commitment to meet regularly with colleagues to unpack the wealth of information and knowledge at our disposal and to select what is most essential and helpful to maintaining and enhancing our lifeworld. We will want to honor in the process our unique identity and culture, our power and potential as human beings and our commitment to purpose—which is always—how will this lead to improving the quality of life for myself and everybody else around me?

Mindful inquiry is an approach that takes into consideration all of these things. It emphasizes the importance of the mindful self; tolerance and the ability to inhabit multiple perspectives; the intention to alleviate suffering; and the notion of clearing space, openness and underlying awareness.[10] We engage in Shared Mindful Inquiry to examine and analyze important topics related to teaching, content area expertise, social justice and equity, and to identify ways that we can improve and adapt our practice.

Mindful Inquiry is unique in that it combines knowledge from critical theory, phenomenology, hermeneutics and Buddhism. It is not important to have an in-depth knowledge of each of these disciplines; we just need to know that it is a holistic, integrated approach. Here is a chart outlining the essential details (Figure 5.3):

Critical Theory	▪ Focuses on liberation, freedom and critical consciousness ▪ Builds knowledge and skills to critique and challenge structures, institutions and systems that perpetuate inequality
Phenomenology	▪ Involves the examination of consciousness and knowledge of the world through awareness of inner experience ▪ Builds knowledge and skills to pay attention to and learn from personal, first-hand experience
Hermeneutics	▪ Emphasizes the understanding and interpretation of texts ▪ Builds knowledge and skills to analyze texts in order to understand how language, symbols and historical context influence knowledge
Buddhism	▪ Focuses on how the processes of the mind and our state of being can create a distorted sense of reality ▪ Builds knowledge and skills to train the mind in order to improve our human nature which relieves suffering

FIGURE 5.3 Essential Elements of Mindful Inquiry.

Most learning organizations have a built in structure that fosters inquiry and shared collaboration amongst colleagues. In schools, we call this a Professional Learning Community (PLC). Shared Mindful Inquiry is a framework and protocol to organize this type of collaborative inquiry. From John Dewey on, theorists have argued that we learn from the past through cycles of action and reflection that lead to new action,[11] and this thinking continues to influence PLCs across the country. When choosing Shared Mindful Inquiry, we are taking a different approach. The goal of this model is *to learn from a future that has not yet happened and discover our role in making sure this future comes to pass.*[12]

Take a moment to review the graphic of the *Shared Mindful Inquiry Cycle*, followed by the *Guiding Questions* for each stage. The details such as norms and processes for each session are determined by the group on the first day. Notice that Contemplative Practices remain at the center of our work and should continue on throughout any cycle of Shared Mindful Inquiry (Figure 5.4).

FIGURE 5.4 Shared Mindful Inquiry Cycle.

Shared Mindful Inquiry Guiding Questions

Envisioning	• Envision the future, establish a vision for your field or local context • Identify the benefits of this vision • Describe in detail the elements and characteristics of the vision • Describe how people experience this future reality emotionally, intellectually and spiritually
Observing Experience	• What emotions and feelings come to mind when you think about this future? • What fears or concerns come to mind? • What about this vision motivates you and inspires you? • Who do you think is responsible for the vision? • What are the practical implications of this vision? What did it take to make it happen? • What parts of this vision do you think are out of reach or outside your current sphere of influence?
Analyzing Texts	• What books or resources can help us explore this vision? • What technical knowledge or information is required? • Is there evidence of or examples of this vision anywhere in the world? • How can we organize our investigation so that we can capture the most important ideas?
Emerging Ideas	• What have we learned about this vision? • What patterns or trends do we notice? • What is important? • What challenges surfaced?
Accepting Responsibility	• What are we doing now that goes against this vision? • How can we prepare for this vision? • What is one thing I can do in my role to make sure this vision comes to pass? • What support will I need?
Reflecting	• What did we learn from this process? • What are our next steps? • How will we support each other moving forward?

Shared Mindful Inquiry Instructions

Preparation

- ◆ You will need to organize a small group of three to six people who will meet regularly over an extended period of time. The person who organizes the group will act as a facilitator.
  - Aim to meet once a week or bimonthly.
  - A cycle of inquiry can extend over several months or it can be a few weeks. You will need a minimum commitment of six 90-min sessions, one for each stage of the cycle. Be flexible and modify as needed.
- ◆ Determine a place to meet and set a regular meeting time.
  - You will need a round table or a circle of chairs.
  - Any changes in location and time should be agreed upon.
  - If possible, send an email reminder with details.
- ◆ Materials
  - Shared Mindful Inquiry Cycle and Guiding Questions;
  - Journal;
  - Texts (For Analyzing Texts Stage);
  - Computer;
  - Timer.

Purpose, Norms and Protocols

- ◆ Set expectations for time and participation.
  - Each member agrees to individually engage in Contemplation and Meditation throughout the duration of the cycle.
  - All members keep a journal to track experience.
- ◆ Establish purpose.
  - Learning from a possible future;
  - Envisioning what it's like to have solved a problem of practice.
- ◆ Determine roles and responsibilities.
  - Facilitator, fixed or rotating;
  - Notetaker;
  - Time manager.
- ◆ Go over Norms for Conscientious Engagement.

Envisioning

- Choose a focus area by thinking about an idea or vision that would improve schools, the system and/or society.
- Imagine the idea/vision has already come to pass. Now you want to explore this future reality, examine what happened, the process it took to get there and the outcomes.
- Refer to Emergence Strategy 3. Envisioning and Imagination for ideas.
- Imagine a future where teachers make highly competitive salaries. The question might be, how have competitive teacher salaries improved schools and society?
- Plan for contemplative practices and journaling on the question.

Observing Experience

- Refer to Authentic Presence Strategy 1. Contemplation and Meditation.
- Engage in Contemplation and Meditation to reflect on first-hand experience related to the topic.
- Share journal entries.
- Plan to bring in a text related to the topic.

Analyzing Texts

- Review text selections. As a group, choose one.
- Refer to Emergence Strategy 3. Wisdom Traditions and Philosophy for text analysis.
- Each member takes a copy of remaining text selections to read before next session.

Emerging Ideas

- Share journal entries.
- Discuss trends and patterns.
- Identify two to three resonating ideas.
- Plan for Contemplation and Meditation and journaling.

Accepting Responsibility

- Share journal entries.
- Identify and share one action that you agree to apply to your practice.

♦ Discuss and plan for a closing ritual to complete the cycle.
♦ Refer to Freedom Strategy 2. Rituals and Ceremonies.
♦ Plan to journal about one action and your early findings.

Reflecting

♦ Share and discuss final journal entries on action and findings.
♦ Prepare and engage in the closing ritual.

Connecting Strategy to Disposition

Curious

♦ How does this protocol channel energy and arouse curiosity?
♦ In what ways might Shared Mindful Inquiry feel difficult or limiting?
♦ How might indulging in or satisfying our curiosity create problems for us?

Strategy 4. Channeling Energy

> Energy is the absolute source of all inspiration and the impetus behind all personal and social transformation or social movement.[13]

The rise of teacher empowerment and ethical leadership, the growing interest in pooling resources and building coalitions, and the focus on collective impact to transform the school system are promising. And yet we have a right to feel cautious. Will this time be different? Are we working together for the same thing? How can we sustain the movement?

A few years ago, I was invited to participate on a diversity task force. The organization had been struggling with this topic for years. In spite of their efforts, they were unable to recruit and retain talented educators from diverse backgrounds, nor create an inclusive and equitable environment across the organization. At first, I was undecided whether I should participate. The task force was voluntary and led by a young woman with a background in finance. Why hadn't they created a formal structure with sanctioned time and a budget? Why hadn't they chosen someone to lead the effort with credibility and expertise? I ended up attending several meetings but as I suspected, the level of participation fell short and the overall experience was discouraging. Although there were moments of enthusiasm and free-flowing ideas, like many other initiatives of this kind, we ended up feeling tired, frustrated and unconvinced that anything substantial would come out of it.

Teams function and thrive off energy. Energy is a source that comes from each individual and from the collective sum of energy of the group. Energy levels fluctuate depending on the flow of energy within and between individuals. All intersubjective systems maintain their order through some type of energy metabolism.[14]

When we become aware of our energy, and how energy is metabolized in relationships and groups, we can make better choices that maximize individual potential and increase group productivity. We can also see where energy is stuck or power is abused, creating imbalance. Part of the work of a Master Teacher is being able to identify behaviors and variables in the environment that drain energy or, conversely, infuse us with power. Also, understanding how one individual can influence the flow of energy in a group. For example, if you have a cold and spent the whole day working with students and filling out paperwork, you are likely to have a low level of energy when you show up to the weekly team meeting. This level of energy walks in the door with you and begins to interact and combine with the collective sum of energy already present in the room. If several members of the team are also unhealthy or tired, then imagine the total sum of energy we are dealing with. On the other hand, if several members of the team just came back from vacation or had two free periods before the meeting, then the type of interaction and power dynamics in that space will be completely different.

Another influence we need to keep in mind is the collective sum of pain of every individual fills the space around us.[15] Collective suffering, guilt or shame of a whole group impacts the field of energy. Trauma and negative emotions not fully faced or seen in the moment they arise leave remnants.[16] For example, if you walk into a school in a distressed neighborhood that has suffered the impact of racism and disenfranchisement, then the energy in that space can either feel stuck and dejected or conversely, infused with passion, purpose and a strong sense of urgency. The latter will depend greatly on how far the school is in the restorative process.

We can learn about energy metabolism of groups by thinking about energy metabolism in an individual. Think back to our exploration of the chakras in Chapter 1. Remember how for yoga, we thought about the flow of energy in our body and explored where energy might be stuck and imbalanced? An imbalance in the Solar Plexus chakra, for instance, manifests as anger, fear, apathy and powerlessness. It is the same when we think about an intersubjective social system such as relationships, groups and cultural entities.

Thinking about the level of energy of each individual, thinking about the energy generated by teams or looking at the flow of energy throughout the organization are all associated with this strategy. Is there one source of power or is power distributed evenly? Where is the organization stuck and out of balance? How can we free up energy to make way for something new? All of these questions are important for managing and sustaining change and implementing new ideas for equity.

Activities

1. Fields of Energy Analysis

Purpose: To consider indicators of group energy, engagement and power dynamics

Overview: Participants observe a meeting and use a tool to assess energy and power dynamics

- ◆ You will need access to a work group meeting or gathering.
  - A work group can be a team, a PLC, a committee, a board, task force or any other convening where there is a shared purpose.
  - If possible, choose a work group that is outside your organization or domain.

- Review the Assessing for Energy and Power Dynamics tool on the next page.
- Plan to meditate for 5–10 min before attending
- Attend the meeting and observe.
  - Sit in an inconspicuous corner without drawing attention to yourself.
  - Have your tool with you so that you can refer to the indicators.
  - Mark the tool.
  - Consider taking notes in the margin to help you remember details.
- Thank the group before leaving.
- When you are alone, reflect and analyze. Consider the following questions:
  - What was challenging or surprising about this activity?
  - How could you tell the difference between an individual's level of energy and the energy of the group as a whole?
  - What did you learn about energy and power dynamics?
  - What would be one suggestion you would offer the group to either improve engagement, realize potential or increase productivity?

2. Field Independence Research

Purpose: To consider how we can sustain and channel our energy wisely in challenging environments

Overview: Participants pay attention to their energy and the field of energy of their workplace and explore self-care strategies with colleagues

- You will need a partner and a timer.
- Both participants agree to document 2 days in their life, paying attention to their level of energy, and come back together to share findings.
  - Set a day for the research and the day to regroup.
  - You can do this activity in a larger group as long as there is an even number to break off into pairs.
- Review the Field Independence Research tool on the next page and go over the following instructions:

- Time: Estimate start and end time. It does not have to be exact.
- Location: Be specific. For example, my office, the hallway, gym, front porch, classroom, in the car in traffic.
- Activity and Description: Describe the purpose and what took place.
- People: Who was involved? What is the role or relationship?
- Energy: Determine your level of energy on a scale of 1–5, with 1 being low-energy and 5 being the highest.
- Energy is defined as a feeling of strength, vitality and power, and the ability to engage actively or exert effort.

◆ Regroup with your partner. Take out the two completed tools. Take turns sharing information about the experience. Set the timer for 8 min.
- Tell each other about the 2 days. Were they typical or unique in some way?
- How did you feel using the tool?
- What was challenging about the process?
- What did you appreciate about the experience?

◆ Now, switch your tools with your partner. Analyze. Set the timer for 5 min.
- What do you notice?
- What activities showed the lowest energy levels?
- What activities resulted in the highest energy levels?
- Do you see any patterns?
- Can you make any inferences about fields of energy?

◆ Share your analysis with your partner. Set the timer for 8 min.
◆ Together, consider entry points and self-care strategies to conserve or channel energy wisely. Set the timer for 10 min.
- An entry point is an indicator that an area may require further examination or exploration, such as a possible imbalance or opportunity for growth or improvement.
- Self-care strategies may include modifying the amount of time spent on an activity, change in location, disengaging with a person or situation to gain perspective.

◆ Conclude by thanking your partner.

Assessing for Energy and Power Dynamics Tool

Reflect on each statement. By using the indicators, assess the group's level of energy and power dynamics throughout the meeting

1. Each member demonstrates enthusiasm

   Strongly disagree   Disagree   Not sure   Agree   Strongly agree

2. Each member understands how the work of the group addresses an issue of significance

   Strongly disagree   Disagree   Not sure   Agree   Strongly agree

3. Each member appears authentic, present and focused

   Strongly disagree   Disagree   Not sure   Agree   Strongly agree

4. Communication is respectful and empowering

   Strongly disagree   Disagree   Not sure   Agree   Strongly agree

5. Information is shared openly

   Strongly disagree   Disagree   Not sure   Agree   Strongly agree

6. There are norms and structures to encourage deliberation

   Strongly disagree   Disagree   Not sure   Agree   Strongly agree

7. Questions are encouraged and responded to with clarity

Strongly disagree   Disagree   Not sure   Agree   Strongly agree

8. Leadership responsibilities are distributed and shared

Strongly disagree   Disagree   Not sure   Agree   Strongly agree

9. Each member takes responsibility for something and understands how they will be recognized or compensated for the effort

Strongly disagree   Disagree   Not sure   Agree   Strongly agree

10. The group is open and receptive to new ideas

Strongly disagree   Disagree   Not sure   Agree   Strongly agree

11. There is a process to examine new ideas to determine how they align with shared values and how they incorporate prior knowledge and wisdom in the field

Strongly disagree   Disagree   Not sure   Agree   Strongly agree

12. There is evidence that new ideas have been successfully integrated in the past

Strongly disagree   Disagree   Not sure   Agree   Strongly agree

Field Independence Research Tool

Time	Place	Activity & Description	People	Level of Energy 1–5
Example 10:15–11:30	Principal's office	Impromptu morning meeting, discussed emergency dismissal schedule, guard and principal had a disagreement about procedure	Principal, Assistant Principal and Security Guard	2

Connecting Strategy to Disposition

Powerful

- ♦ What did you learn about power dynamics?
- ♦ When do you feel powerful? When do you feel powerless?
- ♦ Why would you want power in your practice?
- ♦ How might images of powerful people in the media and politics influence our beliefs about power?

Assessing for Barriers

All human beings are driven by curiosity and the search for wisdom and knowledge. We gravitate to learning experiences that help us understand the purpose of life and the nature of our existence, in other words, learning that raises consciousness. In the first domain, we begin to explore the dynamic nature of our self and our psyche—that which is both material and nonmaterial. In the second domain, we turn our attention to the complex nature of relationships, groups and power—again, encountering layers of subtle and nuanced dynamics. In the last domain, we see how when we bring mindfulness and social justice together, we are dealing with subjective and intersubjective experience in such a way that there is an eruption of new energy and waves of intense emotion. It is the natural push and pull of whole change and transformation. The discomfort we experience is a good sign that we are learning, growing, evolving into something different. It is in fact the birth of something new and with it, comes labor pains.

Power Dynamics and Critical Consciousness

As we discussed earlier, critical consciousness involves an awareness of the intersectionality of factors that contribute to and influence a person's standing and status in society. Unfair power dynamics that have been embedded into our norms, structures, institutions and laws that ensure members of a particular identity group have more power than others, influence relationships in subtle and nuanced ways. The complexity of this work is staying open and receptive to working with people from all backgrounds while also remaining vigilant to attitudes and behaviors that are indicative of oppression. This may mean learning how to challenge or confront an individual or group about a perceived imbalance or abuse in power with gentleness and compassion and communicating a unwavering commitment to the restorative process. It also means learning how to expand our perception of fairness to include the past, present and future rather than seeing fairness as fixed and only pertaining to conditions set at the time. In other words, thinking about how to be responsive to the collective suffering of a group, while also taking into account what is happening right now. Equity in practice is not about seeing everyone as the same or giving everyone the same treatment. It is about seeing the whole person, and the whole history of a people, responding in kindness, and providing what they need to lead a healthy and productive life with dignity.

Activity

Take a moment to think about the learning and activities from this chapter and fill out this chart by considering potential barriers and next steps. At the start of the chapter, I shared a list of barriers including cynicism, egotism, complacency and fatigue. This is not an exhaustive list. Trust yourself and your feelings as you process your learning. Use the example for guidance.

Strategy	Potential Barrier/s	Next Steps
Envisioning and Imagination	Example: Cynicism	Think about a success. What was the original idea? How did it grow?
Wisdom Traditions and Philosophy		
Shared Mindful Inquiry		
Channeling Energy		

Application to Practice: Performance Assessment and Coaching Tool

The following is a *tool* to help you assess, monitor and coach for performance. It can be used with individuals and groups.

Performance Assessment and Coaching Tool

Name/s	Date
Domain	Strategy

Activities and Purpose		
Insights	**Application to Practice**	**Observing Experience**
		Level of Energy/Agency ❏ High ❏ Medium ❏ Low
Emerging Ideas		**Relevance**
Next Steps		
Support Needed		

Checking In

Go back to your Initial Self-Assessment. Review your answers to Part III. Emergence. Reflect on the following questions:

- What are three things you learned about Emergence?
- Why is Transpersonal Awareness and Agency important?
- What aspect of this domain do you want to concentrate on moving forward?
- How would you describe the driving force behind your professional practice?
- Do you think your level of energy and agency matches others in your field? Why or why not?
- What questions do you still have?

Notes

1 Rios, R. (2017) *Teacher Agency for Equity: A Framework for Conscientious Engagement*. Routledge, New York, p. 193.

2 Edwards, B. (1999) *The New Drawing on the Right Side of the Brain*. Penguin Putnam Inc., New York, p. 5.

3 Edwards, B. (1999) *The New Drawing on the Right Side of the Brain*. Penguin Putnam Inc., New York, p. 39.

4 Siegel, D. (2007) *The Mindful Brain, Mind Your Brain*. W. W. Norton & Company Inc., New York & London, pp. 45–46.

5 Edwards, B. (1999) *The New Drawing on the Right Side of the Brain*. Penguin Putnam Inc., New York.

6 Adapted from Futures Wheel Activity created by Jerome Glenn, 1972, https://www.mindtools.com/pages/article/futures-wheel.htm.

7 Rios, R. (2017) *Teacher Agency for Equity: A Framework for Conscientious Engagement*. Routledge, New York, p. 98.

8 Rice, L. (2006) *What Was It Like? Teaching History and Culture through Young Adult Literature*. Teachers College Press, Columbia University, New York, p. 11.

9 Rios, R. (2017) *Teacher Agency for Equity: A Framework for Conscientious Engagement*. Routledge, New York, p. 54.

10 Bentz, V.M. and Shapiro, J.J. (1998) *Mindful Inquiry in Social Research*. Sage Publications, Thousand Oaks, CA, pp. 36–39.

11   Senge, P., Scharmer, C.O., Jaworski, J. and Flowers, B.S. (2004) *Presence: Human Purpose and the Field of the Future*. Crown Publishing, New York, p. 86.
12   Senge, P., Scharmer, C.O., Jaworski, J. and Flowers, B.S. (2004) *Presence: Human Purpose and the Field of the Future*. Crown Publishing, New York, p. 86.
13   Rios, R. (2017) *Teacher Agency for Equity: A Framework for Conscientious Engagement*. Routledge, New York, p. 101.
14   McIntosh, S. (2007) *Integral Consciousness and the Future of Evolution*. Paragon House, St. Paul, MN, p. 26.
15   Rossiter, A. (2006) *Developing Spiritual Intelligence. The Power of You*. O Books, Winchester.
16   Tolle, E. (2005) *A New Earth: Awakening to Your Life's Purpose*. A Plume Book, Penguin Group, New York, p. 141.

6

The Unicorn Point

Scratch a good teacher and you will find a moral purpose.[1]

Michael Fullan

After a pleasant first interview for a role in a national organization that trains educational leaders for equity, I was informed that the second step in the 8-week-long process was to complete a 4-hour performance task. A one-page instruction sheet with links to models and tools commonly used by career development coaches appeared in an email. The task was to outline how I would integrate, adapt or recreate elements from the model for use in leadership coaching and virtual learning. This was not the first time I had encountered this type of request. Over a 9-month period, I had written numerous letters to organizations and universities; completed countless online applications; submitted several writing samples; and completed a range of performance tasks including data analysis, feedback on lesson plans and videos of teachers teaching, designing a training outline, facilitating a virtual Professional Learning Community, designing a PowerPoint presentation and speaking at length on a variety of education topics. For one job, I was asked to conduct a one-way, online video interview involving speaking into a camera with no live person on the other end and I refused. This time, I sat at my desk and contemplated. When is enough enough? I focused on my breath and detached myself from my pain and frustration and began to see these experiences for what they were, insight into a disturbing trend. Recruitment and hiring practices in education had become alienating and dehumanizing. I sent an email informing the organization that I would no longer provide original ideas or designs as part of the interview process, but would share samples of my work from my portfolio. The next morning, I got a reply explaining their commitment to an equitable process and their need to see work as it relates to that role specifically. I was not advanced to the next level.

In a field where the majority of teachers are white and teaching diverse students, where the percentage of black or Hispanic public-school principals has barely budged for more than 25 years;[2] where, of all full-time faculty in degree-granting post-secondary institutions in the fall of 2016, only 2% were Hispanic females,[3] it is easy for me to question our hiring and recruitment strategy. What criteria are we using? What are the norms, procedures and systems that bar diverse talent from getting leadership and teaching positions in the field of education? What do current trends in hiring practices say about what we value in education?

Yesterday, my daughter came home waving the AP European History essay rubric in the air. She pointed to the last item on the list. "See this? This is what my teacher calls, the unicorn point." I looked up from my writing. "He says the unicorn point is hard to explain, but it's given to a student that captures the essential elements of writing, plus, demonstrates a distinctive style or approach that makes the reader understand the bigger picture, the big understandings…" While my daughter rambled on trying to explain the unicorn point, my heart filled with joy and gratitude for her teacher who had the courage to talk about unicorns in the context of AP European History.

All of our effort and ideas do not matter in education unless we pay attention to the unicorn point, that which makes human experience dynamic and enjoyable. How we recruit and hire talent, what criteria we use, how we communicate with individuals and how we value each other's time and livelihood—all of these things demonstrate how much we cherish human beings and our work in education. If we want Master Teachers from all backgrounds to teach our children and we want well-rounded, caring, talented, hard-working, mindful individuals to choose a life of teaching—we need to take a long, hard look at how we approach talent and human resources. In this last activity, we begin to think about transforming hiring and recruitment practices into dynamic, human experience. What is our unicorn point?

Activity

Building a Team

Purpose: To consider the criteria and process for building a dynamic team committed to mindfulness and social justice

Overview: Participants review the three domains of Peak Learning Experience, develop the criteria for candidates and consider the interview process

- ◆ You will need the *Three Domains for Peak Learning Experience Framework*, chart paper, a marker, a timer and a group of three to five participants.
  - Choose a role you would like to focus on for the activity: teacher, faculty member, guidance counselor, principal, director, etc.
    - ◆ The precise role is less important than exploring the process and the rubric. Later, you will adapt both to your specific needs and context.
- ◆ Individually, review the Three Domains for Peak Learning Experience Framework. Set the timer for 5 min.
- ◆ Choose a facilitator and writer for the group.
  - Draw a T-Chart.
  - Write the role on the top.
  - Label the left column **Criteria** and the right column **Evidence**.
- ◆ As a group, begin to brainstorm the selection criteria and what evidence might demonstrate these criteria on a resume. Set the timer for 15 min.
  - For example, if the criteria is that we want someone who can integrate culture and identity studies into the program (Strategy #3 in the first domain), then evidence might include work experience, a major in college or scholarly articles on the topic of culturally relevant pedagogy.

- If the group determines that the criteria cannot be demonstrated on a resume, mark the item with an **X**. For example, authenticity. Can authenticity show up on a resume?
- Keep the conversation grounded in the Three Domains framework, thinking about the strategies, tools, dispositions and barriers.

◆ Now think about the interview process for candidates. Break into pairs. Set the timer for 15 min.
- What would the process entail?
- How long should the interview process take?
- What would be an adequate salary?
- Who would be involved?
- What questions would be asked?

◆ Come back together as a whole group and discuss. Set the timer for 7 min.
- What did we learn by going through this process?
- How much of our decision-making was based on personal or past experience?
- What challenges do you anticipate when changing hiring practices?

◆ Conclude by taking a few minutes to quietly reflect and write. Set the timer for 6 min
- Why do you think there is an imbalance in the demographics in the education sector?
- What do you think makes for a positive and effective hiring experience?
- What concerns you about changing how we recruit and hire teachers and leaders?
- In your opinion, how would you describe the "the unicorn point" in the teaching profession?

Notes

1 Fullan, M. (1993) *Change Forces: Probing the Depths of Education Reform*. The Falmer Press, Taylor & Francis, Bristol, PA, p. 21.
2 Anderson, M. (2016) Where Are All the Principals of Color, *The Atlantic*. Retrieved from www.theatlantic.com/education/archive/2016/06/principals-of-color/488006/
3 The National Center for Education Statistics, Fast Facts. Retrieved from https://nces.ed.gov/fastfacts/display.asp?id=61

Afterword

We cannot solve the world's problems, but we can resolve value conflicts and imbalances in our own life and our professional practice. Policies and practices that distort the role of teachers and the purpose of schools, creating a culture of fear, competition and dualism have no place in our future. We are wired for basic goodness and altruism, and born with a natural drive for truth, wisdom and respect for humanity. We know our suffering, and only by attending to and relieving our suffering, can we begin to model a new way of being, a new standard for education and society. It is time, and time is on our side.

It is important to see yourself as a Master Teacher in training and to seek out the wisdom, support and guidance of masters, who regardless of their title and position in society, will be put in your path to help you move ahead in your development. Learn to recognize them. The field of education continues to privilege individuals who perform well in the tradition of the Academy and who make a living on college campuses and university settings, with all that implies. The university is not the official home of masters. The dearth of Latino, African American, Native American and Asian faculty within these institutions is an indicator that the knowledge base we have always relied on is narrow and limited. Some might argue that our first Master Teacher, is the one closest to home.

In order to do this work with dignity, we have to be clever with our time and how we manage ourselves in the real world. We want to be active participants in the evolution of our profession, but there may be times when we find ourselves unemployed or exiled from the work we love. At all times, we must continue to work on ourselves and our craft knowing that each phase of our life lends itself to mastery, in so far we accept this as our greatest and noblest charge. We must make a commitment to train our mind, refine our attention and seek understanding and compassion. Most importantly, conscientious engagement at all times.

We all want to be seen, to be loved and to be useful. We all want to make a difference. We are only agents of change when we are self-actualized and conscious of our interdependence; when we recognize that our individual experience of sanity is inherently linked to our vision of a good human society.[1]

If you would like to learn more, continue the conversation, share your experience or inquire about how to bring this work into your organization, visit www.ConscientiousEngagement.com.

Superpowers

Here is a list of Superpowers that I have collected. Feel free to add to this list.

Appreciating nature
Baking
Being myself
Being with children
Bravery
Breathing
Building things
Building on strengths
Building relationships
Collaborating with colleagues
Communicating with animals
Connecting with teenagers
Contemplation
Cooking
Dancing
Drawing what I see
Eating well
Empathizing
Encouraging people to think creatively and critically
Expressing myself with words

Facilitating conversations
Finding humor
Finding the good in others
Freedom education
Gardening
Gathering information
Gift giving
Growing food
Helping others
Holding people's attention
Inspiring people
Learning
Learning languages
Listening
Living well
Loving
Making art
Making complicated concepts easy to understand
Making connections between ideas
Making friends

Making people feel important
Making people feel
    comfortable
Making personal connections
Making people laugh
Managing
Mentoring
Music
Networking
Observing
Observing nature
Organizing
Philosophizing
Planning
Planning events
Playing music
Prayer
Reading
Seeing talent
Singing
Smiling
Solving problems
Speaking in front of groups
Sports
Staying calm
Swimming
Taking care of others
Talking
Teaching
Teaching math in culturally
    relevant ways
Thinking about solutions to
    problems
Understanding kids
Walking
Writing

Note

1   Trungpa, C. (1984) *Shambhala: The Sacred Path of the Warrior.*
     Shambhala Publications, Inc. Boston, MA. p. 126

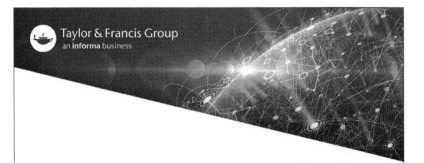

Made in the USA
Middletown, DE
30 April 2019